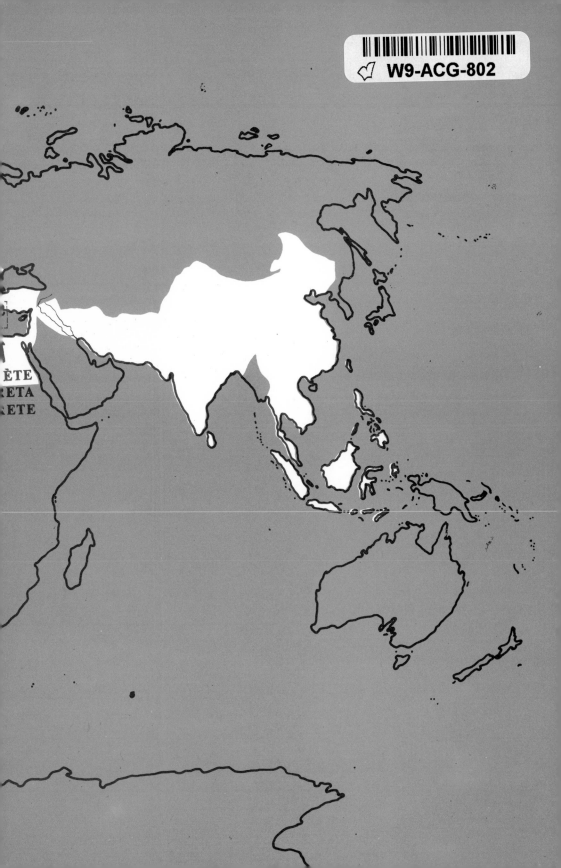

In the same series:

ARCHAEOLOGIA MVNDI

Series prepared under the direction of Jean Marcadé, Professor of Archaeology at the University of Bordeaux.

NICOLAS PLATON

CRETE

Translated from the Greek

64 illustrations in colour;
61 illustrations in black-and-white

THE WORLD PUBLISHING COMPANY
CLEVELAND AND NEW YORK

CONTENTS

PREFACE

The discovery of the Minoan civilization on the site of Knossos marked an important date in the annals of archaeology. Today Crete is again in the news: since 1960 a lively controversy has been raging round the chronology of the Linear B tablets brought to light by Evans. At Zakro, at the eastern end of the large island, a new palace has been discovered, and is providing a vast amount of fresh material for study because it was the first that had not been pillaged. This unhoped-for discovery will not only add to the many art treasures in the Museum of Heracleion but will enable Cretan archaeologists to check their latest conclusions and to make further progress in their field.

In this series we are attempting to examine the changing facets of archaeology in its many varied domains. We have asked the excavator of Zakro to discuss the problems, methods, and results of Minoan archaeology. This he has done with the assurance and competence born of long experience. He has dealt with the problems that have arisen and shown their logical sequence. He has given us an insight into the excavation in all its material and technical aspects and into the responsibilities involved. Finally he has examined the results of this work, in which many nations have taken part and from which emerges a clear picture of the amazingly sophisticated civilization that flourished in the kingdoms of Minos, Sarpedon, Rhadamanthus and Idomeneus during the second millenium B.C.

J. M.

We should like to thank the following for their valuable cooperation:
H. E. Mr. Angelos Vlachos, Minister Plenipotentiary, Director of the Depart-
ment for Cultural Affairs, Athens; Mr. Joannes Kontis, Director General of
the Service for the Preservation of Ancient Monuments, Athens; Mr. Stylianos
Alexiou, Superintendent of Antiquities, Heracleion; Mr. Demetrios Papaefstra-
tiou, Secretary General of the Greek National Tourist Organization, Athens;
Mr. Aleco G. Coromilas,· Mr. Theophilos Frangopoulos, Mr. Demosthenes
Pouris, Directors of the Greek National Tourist Organization, Athens;
Mrs. Fany Lambadariou, former Head of the Publicity Department of the
Greek National Tourist Organization, Athens; Mr. Andreas Vlachakis,
Information Office of the Greek National Tourist Organization, Heracleion;
Mr. Thomas Phanourakis, Heracleion.

We should also like to express our thanks to Mrs. Helen Vlachos, Athens,
Professor Angelos Angelopoulos, Geneva and Professor Gerassimos Patroni-
kolas, Athens, whose advice and help on all our publications concerning Greece
are always most valuable.

INTRODUCTION

While the prehistoric archaeology of the Mediterranean world is a recent science, barely a century old, the prehistoric archaeology of Crete — called Minoan archaeology by Evans—is some thirty years younger. Yet in the relatively short time available, scholars have brought to light an ancient civilization that had been completely unknown before although it was one of the greatest in the world and lies at the root of our western civilization. Minoan archaeology has become a science in its own right, with its own working methods and its own basic problems; it has overcome its initial difficulties and is making a substantial contribution to the sum of human knowledge.

Many scholars from various countries have explored the soil of Crete and studied the problems of the civilization discovered there. They have published many books and learned articles, but in most of them they use technical terms that are unintelligible to the layman. This study is intended to give the educated general reader a survey of the achievements of Cretan archaeology, of its problems, its methods and the main conclusions it has reached. It is not easy to do this in the limited space available, but we hope to arouse the reader's interest and encourage him to pursue the subject on his own.

The author has worked in Crete for some thirty years and has been personally acquainted with almost all the noted archaeologists who have worked there. He has also organized the museum at Heracleion where the main finds from the excavations are housed, and has a wide experience of the problems relating to the preservation of ancient monuments. He is therefore eminently qualified to give us this general outline of Minoan archaeology.

We shall deal mainly with the chief problems that have preoccupied the experts, the methods they have used during their investigations and for the restoration and preservation of the finds, their presentation in museums, and the final publication of the work. We shall deal briefly with the achievements of Minoan archaeology, its historical significance, and the developments that may be expected in the future.

THE PROBLEMS

I

By the end of last century a decisive step had been taken in the field of archaeology. Thanks to the enthusiasm and intuition of an imaginative amateur, a brilliant and complex civilization was brought to light in the Aegean basin. Moreover, its principal centres seemed to coincide with those that had figured prominently in the Homeric epics. Between 1870 and 1890, the spade of Heinrich Schliemann uncovered "Troy of the broad streets", "Mycenae rich in gold", "walled Tiryns" and Minyan Orchomenos all of which yielded invaluable treasures that pre-dated by several centuries the "golden age" of Greece.

The enigma of the earliest discoveries

From Mycenae to Knossos

Archaeologists were dumbfounded; they could not understand how the very existence of such a highly developed civilisation could have remained unsuspected until then. This raised the first problem: what were the roots of this civilization, which was called Mycenaean after the area where it had flourished? For a time scholars sought its origins in the civilization of Phoenicia which was itself only imperfectly known. A number of similarities between the two seemed to justify this approach.

Meanwhile, in the central and eastern part of Crete, isolated remains of a very ancient civilization were brought to light by amateurs and small groups of archaeologists or discovered simply by chance. They were very different from the remains found at Mycenae, yet seemed related to them and even to predate them. This suggested that the newly discovered civilization might have originated in Crete. Schliemann himself had already become interested in the Knossos region and intended to undertake large-scale excavations there, but his negotiations to obtain permission from the

Turkish authorities were unsuccessful. At the site of Knossos, a local amateur—by a strange coincidence camed Minos Kalokairinos—had already excavated the first storerooms of the palace, with their rows of jars still in place; and in 1894, Arthur Evans appeared on the scene, seeking the solution to another problem that was of considerable importance.

On many small artistic objects from Crete, and especially on seal-stones, the British scholar had noticed strange hieroglyphic markings differing from the Egyptian ones. He thought that this proved the existence in the Mediterranean basin of a very ancient "pre-Phoenician" script that was certainly the oldest in Europe; it was used chiefly in Crete where he expected therefore to find the traces of a correspondingly advanced civilization. The specimens he collected during his first visit to the island seemed to support this hypothesis, and he hoped that large-scale excavations would confirm his theory and provide many further examples of the script. The start of the excavation was delayed by interminable negotiations with the Turks for the purchase of the site, and in fact nothing was achieved until after the island was given self-rule in 1899. At the same time, an Italian mission led by Frederico Halbherr and Luigi Pernier was excavating Phaestos, a prehistoric site mentioned by Homer and situated in the southern part of Central Crete, on the fertile plain of Messara.

Discovery of the Minoan civilization
From the start amazing discoveries were made, and Greek, American, and later French investigators began to explore the whole of central and eastern Crete (western Crete seemed less promising). The main discoveries were made during the first decade of this century, but work has continued actively ever since with important results and a constant improvement of methods. Vast multi-storeyed palaces, villas, farmsteads, districts of populous and well-organized cities, harbour installations, networks of roads crossing the island from end to end, organized places of worship and planned burial

2

3

4

5

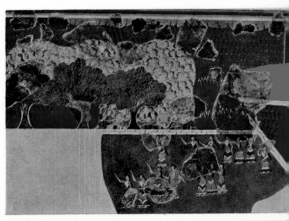

10 11

13

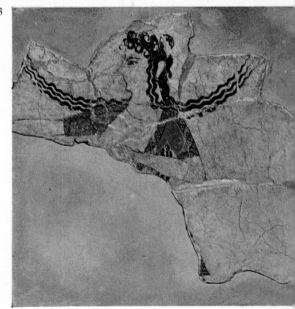

grounds were brought to light. The museum at Heracleion was built to house the many valuable objects discovered and now contains a unique collection. From the study of the finds there emerged a picture of the social, political, and religious life of the period. Gradually the various phases in the long development of this civilization could be distinguished and its relations with other ancient cultures clarified. Its geographical and chronological boundaries could be determined. Its character was studied from every angle. The discovery of extensive archives gave rise to a reasonable hope that it might be possible to classify it as a historic, not a prehistoric, civilization once the texts had been deciphered. Finally, abundant material was discovered that throws light both on the Neolithic civilization that preceded it and on its own decline and collapse as a result of internal or external factors. The historical setting began to be outlined with growing clarity although much of the detail still remained obscure.

At the very outset of the major excavations, two basic problems were solved. The Mycenaean civilization did, in fact, have its roots in the Cretan civilization, and the latter had used a system of writing as was shown by the discovery of a great number of inscribed objects. However, as the investigations continued fresh problems were raised, some of which have not been solved satisfactorily to this day.

Problems
The civilization discovered in Crete had undergone a long development and had passed through several successive periods separated from one another by catastrophes of varying importance. After each of these catastrophes life was resumed with some changes but along the same general lines as before. The order and duration of these periods, their individual features, the causes of the successive catastrophes, the reason for changes in forms and the characteristics of each innovation, all these had to be determined. The division into phases and periods was based chiefly on the

development of pottery, of which continuous series were available. This method, however, raised some difficult problems; some styles might have only local reference or be confined to palace products, differing from the style in general use; some conservative districts might retain old forms while others were adopting new ones. There was a danger that different forms might represent parallel developments during one and the same period. What valid criteria could be used to classify the successive ages, periods, and phases? Some archaeologists suggested the progress of metal-working techniques, others the development of pottery, and yet others the principal catastrophes together with the history of the palaces as the main centres from which the civilization had spread. Each of these criteria had some advantages but also considerable disadvantages. By establishing the successive periods a relative chronology could be obtained, but at the same time it was necessary to solve the problem of the absolute chronology in order to obtain a clearer historical perspective. This could only be achieved with the help of clear written evidence or means analogous to those used in establishing the chronologies of the civilizations of Egypt and the East. It would be difficult, too, to establish a chronology that would not have to be revised and rectified in the light of fresh historical knowledge.

The origins

Origin of the people

Research has shown that the Minoan civilization was preceded on the island by a Neolithic one with a long development that was particularly slow in its earliest phases. What were the relations between the Neolithic civilization and the Minoan? The continuity of some Neolithic features suggests that the Minoan civilization gradually developed from it. On the other hand, it might have grown independently despite some Neolithic survivals. The latter seems more likely, for the Minoan civilization clearly was a complex one and altogether different in its character. The relationship between the Neolithic civilization in Crete and that in the other parts of the eastern Mediterranean had to be clarified.

The origin of the Minoan civilization remained a riddle. If it resulted from the arrival of a new racial element, then it had to be established where this new group came from, at what point it appeared on the island, and what kind of civilization it brought with it. The racial group could have been identified from the anthropological remains, but the first excavators paid little attention to these and rarely preserved the bones found in the tombs. If the newcomers belonged to a different racial type from the Neolithic, both types must have coexisted for a time until they gradually formed a mixed type which might be called Eastern Mediterranean.

Origin of the language
A knowledge of the language of the Minoan civilization would help to determine its racial character and its links with other racial groups. Even before the start of the great excavations in Crete, the linguists—especially Kretschmer—had distinguished the existence round the eastern end of the Mediterranean of a pre-Hellenic people, fragments of whose language had survived in some place names and general terms. However, the distribution of these terms suggested the existence of a wider linguistic group that was not confined to Crete alone. This subject raised a series of problems concerning the origin and signifiance of these pre-Hellenic place-names. The solution of these problems might be hastened if, by the decipherment of the older texts, some light could be thrown on the subsequent development of the language.

It is certain that the growth of the Minoan civilization was assisted by its favourable geographical position that made it a crossroads of civilizations.

27

But this does not explain the successive formation of such widely dissimilar civilizations in the same natural setting, nor to what extent the new civilization was shaped or influenced by its environment.

Contacts with other countries
Other centres developed at the eastern end of the Mediterranean at the same time as the Minoan civilization; they seem to have been related to it and may have sprung from a common Mediterranean ethnic root. They included the Cycladic civilization in the islands of the Cyclades, the Trojan with its centre at Troy, and the Helladic civilization in mainland Greece. The Minoans must have had close relations with all these civilizations, especially the Cycladic. Scholars have attempted to analyse these relations, to define the points of contact and assess their consequences. A comparative study of the parallel civilizations would help to correlate their chronologies.

The dynamic and versatile Minoans would naturally have made contact with the great civilizations of Anatolia and Egypt, especially during the period of their expansion. The nature and extent of these contacts, their direct or indirect influence leading to the reciprocal assimilation or adaptation of certain features, the relative chronologies—all these questions have been studied closely. Certain similarities with more distant cultures, e. g., the Sumerian and Proto-Indian, have raised further problems.

The Minoan civilization seemed to differ basically from its great contemporories, although there are some superficial resemblances. The exact nature of these differences and of the features that were original in Minoan culture has been discussed extensively. It was not clear how its character had developed through the centuries, how it had manifested itself, and indeed in what its uniqueness consisted.

The successive catastrophes

Its development could be traced only through a detailed study of each age, period, and phase and of the causes, extent, and consequences of the successive catastrophes on the basis of the evidence yielded by the soil. In order to interpret this evidence it was necessary to take into account not only human factors but also the upheavals of nature, such as earthquakes, volcanic eruptions, landslides, etc. It must be remembered that Crete has been subject to such upheavals from earliest times to the present day. Internal disturbances and foreign invasions, especially during the periods of the great migrations, had also to be considered. It was particularly important to discover the causes of those large-scale catastrophes that were followed by radical changes or the appearance of completely new features. The total destruction of the old and new palaces has naturally been the subject of special study.

In the course of research into the successive phases of Minoan civilization, new and increasingly complex problems have arisen.

The Pre-Palace civilization

From Neolithic to "Proto-Minoan"

Excavations in eastern Crete have shown that, even before the foundation of the great palace centres Minoan civilization had come a long way. On the basis of developments in pottery and of certain stratigraphical observations, scholars have subdivided this early period into three successive phases, Early Minoan I–III—Evans being the main supporter of this classification. But its validity was soon questioned, for in the palaces both at Knossos and Phaestos it was found that the Neolithic was followed immediately by the Pre-Palace civilization; moreover, objects which, according to the classification, should have belonged to successive phases were in fact found side by side. In fact, it was doubtful whether there really had been a Pre-Palace civilization; Franchet, I. Hatzidakis and Aberg had already raised this problem, and Doro Levi undertook extensive research at Phaestos to investigate it more fully.

The sudden progress in arts and techniques
In any case, it was agreed that the so-called Early Minoan or Pre-Palace civilization was anything but primitive. Its art forms were varied and highly developed. But what was the relationship between the figurative styles it gradually perfected and the Neolithic pottery that had preceded them? We might also ask how colour came to be used for decorative purposes and what was the exact link between the dark decorations on a light ground and the light ones on a dark ground.

Towards the end of the period some pottery styles made a limited use of polychrome decoration. Were these forerunners of the later polychrome style of Kamares or were they simply regional examples of it? When was the curved line—especially the spiral—first introduced and where did it come from? When was the potter's wheel first used and in what way?

The introduction of metal, particularly of bronze, marked a turning point, and this has raised many problems for the scholar. It was not known where the raw material came from and whether it was smelted at the mines by special teams sent for that purpose. Deposits of copper-bearing ores might have been found in Crete itself. Nor was it known how bronze working had progressed to the stage of a fully fledged industry. Similar problems arose regarding the sources of precious metal and the technical progress that led to the development of gold and silver work.

The technique of stone-cutting had ancient roots, but it is amazing that such an early age should have produced vessels made from hard polychrome stone in such varied shapes. Many types of local stone were also used and some of these, like steatite, were soft and easy to work. But where did the great variety of hard stones come from and how were they worked?

Ivory was a precious material and easier to work, but it was not known where it came from. The use of ivory together with steatite, for seals, was probably borrowed from neighbouring civilizations. The origin of such outside influences on Pre-Palace art had to be determined.

Seal-carving became a sophisticated art in which patterns of increasing refinement and complexity were evolved. On the seals, too, appear the first examples of writing, but the evolution of writing itself remains obscure. It is possible that it was also used on other materials that were too fragile to survive.

Development of architecture

The discovery of the first pre-palace settlements, mainly in eastern Crete, raised fresh problems. Compared with the Neolithic dwellings, these stout buildings of brick or stone testified to a completely new way of building that was certainly not just a development of earlier methods. This raised the problem of the origin of this new architecture and of its development until the appearance of the palaces. It was also difficult to decide whether the buildings found at the deepest levels beneath the palaces should be described as Pre-Palace or Proto-Palace.

In eastern Crete, the burial grounds contained both small tombs and vast funerary enclosures with inner chambers, while in central Crete—especially in the plain of Messara—the earliest stone-built tholos tombs were brought to light. It was not easy to determine whether these enclosures were exposed to the open air and whether they were places of burial or ossuaries. Nor was it clear whether the circular tombs were properly vaulted or whether they were simply round enclosures. The fact that they were used for many burials, together with the existence of a large number of tholos tombs in the same area, suggests a social organization based on clans. The many charred remains found inside tombs may be evidence of ritual cremation or simply of measures of expediency.

Political, social and religious questions
There was not enough evidence on the social, political, economic and religious life of the Pre-Palace period to enable scholars to form even a general idea of these aspects of the life of the time. The basic features of social organization as found later in the Old and New-Palace periods may already have been in existence. Was the matrilineal factor essential in the organization of the family? Was property held on a feudal basis? Did the heads of families hold political power locally? Was trade based on barter or on an elementary money system? Settlements on small islands and peninsulas and along safe inlets suggest that there was some navigation which would, in any case, be necessary to import raw materials. But it was not certain whether this involved the organization of ports, the building of a merchant fleet, an import and export trade and, later, the establishment of trading posts outside the island. Eastern Crete was ahead of central Crete in this respect, but we do not know whether the Cycladic settlements on the island played any significant part in the development of trade with the eastern Mediterranean.

Some of the religious features were of a type later developed on a large scale. This, however, does not prove conclusively that the basic principles of the Minoan religion—its divinities, its forms and places of worship, the organization of its priesthood—had already been laid down. Religion may still have been based on magic and the vestiges of an ancient totemism.

Finally, scholars had to determine whether the successive catastrophes were caused by geological upheavals or whether they were connected with the final concentration of power in the hands of a few strong local governors who subsequently became kings.

The absolute chronology of the Pre-Palace periods has been approached chiefly through the study of Egyptian influences on stone vases. These influences, however, do not necessarily mean that there were particularly

14

15

16

17

18

19

23

25

close links with Egypt. The obvious resemblance between proto-Minoan and early Oriental seal-engraving may be due to commerce or to a common racial stock.

The Old Palace civilization

Difficulties of investigation

The investigation of the Old Palace levels was a difficult task and yielded little that showed what they actually looked like. It has nevertheless been possible to form a general idea of their appearance and to trace their development through three successive periods. Detailed study has raised a great number of problems, most of which have not yet been solved. It has been difficult to determine which of the remains belonged to each period, for superimposed buildings might be ascribed to separate phases while, in fact, they were separate storeys of the same building; remains of the earliest phase of the New Palaces might be mistaken for buildings from the final phase of the Old Palaces. It was difficult, too, to follow the architectural development of the buildings and to decide whether an overall plan was followed or whether successive additions were made at random; whether earlier remains were demolished to make way for new buildings; whether the monumental character of the palaces was a feature of the final phase alone; and whether the plan of the old palaces was preserved at least in its general lines in the new palaces. These complex, multi-storeyed buildings with their extensive courtyards and their colonnades and porticos bore some resemblance to buildings in the Near East and Anatolia. But these similarities needed to be elucidated, and it was far from certain that the architectural lay-out of the palaces had been introduced to Crete by settlers.

Difficulties in interpretation

Much of the evidence suggested that life in the palaces and in the surrounding cities was fully organized. There certainly were palace workshops
producing pottery of exceptional quality with polychrome decorations.
It was not known how such technical skill had been developed nor why it
was employed until the end for purely decorative purposes. What was the
secret of its charm? Was it widely distributed in the island and beyond it?
It was difficult, too, to determine whether it was subject to influences from
other countries or whether, on the other hand, it exerted an influence on
foreign pottery. Had it remained a palace pottery to the end, while the
production of older, more conservative styles went on concurrently?

Palace art undoubtedly extended into many other fields, such as metal-
working, gem-engraving, seal-engraving, the production of faience and
perhaps even of glass. Little was known of the progress made in these
domains. Few examples of metal work had been found, but the tremendous
development of metal-working has been demonstrated by the hoards of
objects found outside Crete and by the faithful imitation of metal prototypes
in the pottery of Kamares. It was not known how these copies were made
or whether the metal objects found outside Crete were of Cretan origin.
Seal-engraving was practised on hard semi-precious or precious stones, but
the predominance of certain types and forms of seals and the techniques
used had not been explained. Most examples of Cretan hieroglyphic writing
were preserved on these seals, but the same script appeared concurrently on
clay tablets. Was it related to Egyptian hieroglyphic writing and to what
extent had it evolved? It was hoped that these inscriptions might throw some
light on the language in use at the time.

It is probable that Crete had close contacts with the outside world, especially
with the Aegean islands and Egypt, since there is evidence that many
objects were imported from and exported to these countries. What is not
certain, however, is the extent to which these contacts had developed into

a regular system of trade, with the establishment outside Crete of trading posts to deal in essential raw materials. The development of shipping, which could be studied from harbour installations, improved ship-building techniques etc., would also be an indication of the growth of trade.

Gaps in our knowledge

The organization of the palaces as centres of the life of the time presupposes a general social, political, and economic organization. Little light has been shed on this subject because the evidence yielded by the excavations has been inadequate and ambiguous. Was the kingdom already organized on a theocratic basis? Had there been a radical change in the old system of family groups or γένη? We do not know what were the exact relations between the various palace districts and if the three great palace centres that have been discovered—Knossos, Phaestos, and Mallia—were in fact the only ones. Was the role of woman in society as important as in the subsequent New Palace period? Was the organization of trade already controlled by the palace? There are many other problems, especially concerning religion of which very little is known; a form of worship was practised in the palaces, but also in certain caves, and that there were many sanctuaries on mountain tops is shown by the votive offerings and terracotta figurines that have been found there. It seems on the whole that throughout its long development Minoan religion retained its fundamental character as a religion of deified nature.

The end of the Old Palace centres seems to have been sudden, complete and general. What was the terrible catastrophe that caused such total destruction and necessitated a completely fresh start?

The New Palace civilization

An astonishing achievement

In the reconstruction period, Minoan civilization found its full means of expression and its final character was shaped; here the question of how it had acquired its specific originality arose. Although the new palaces continued a development begun by the old palaces, the astonishing form they took raised a whole series of problems. It was not known how they were adapted to their surroundings and equipped to deal with the many practical needs of palace life, how the monumental layout of the site was achieved and how the interior, with its labyrinthine corridors, innumerable rooms and many storeys, was organized. These complex buildings had to fulfil many functions, not only as centres of political administration and as royal residences, but also as temples of the deity. This involved solving a host of problems regarding lighting, drainage, water supply, sanitary installations, etc. The destruction of many of the wooden features and of the perishable coverings made it difficult to reconstruct them, so that many problems arose concerning the nature of the basic framework, the doors, windows, storeys, etc. The surviving fragments of the mural decorations left tantalizing doubts as to the subjects they depicted, their position in the building, and the technique used in their execution. It was definitely established that the palaces were the **centres round** which the whole social, political, religious and economic life of the times revolved. The finest works of art were produced in the royal workshops. It would therefore be important to discover how these workshops were organized, what they produced, how they were equipped and supplied with raw materials, and what were the techniques used in them.

A highly sophisticated art and way of life

Starting from palace production, the whole artistic production of the period had to be examined. A fundamental problem was that of the origin of the new naturalistic styles in pottery. The formation of a new, monumental style, called the Palace Style and imbued with a new spirit also needed explaining. This change was noticeable in other art forms, but it was not known where it came from. Technical accomplishments could be studied from positive evidence, for kilns, pottery workshops, and potter's wheels had been preserved. Terracotta works were used chiefly by the sanctuaries and their stores, and much could be learnt about them from a careful study of their technique, morphology, and symbolism. Less was known about the manufacture of vases and stone tools, but the excavations of several workshops provided some important clues about working methods, raw materials, and tools.

Shaped vessels in stone, and others with relief carving provided information on the techniques of engraving, carving, and inlaying. These could also be studied in minor items such as playthings and toilet articles. The outstanding quality of faience and chryselephantine objects together with the aesthetic and technical problems they raised, also offered a suitable field for study. The greatest difficulties, however, were encountered in connection with metal-working. A whole series of technical problems relating to alloys, processes of lamination, riveting, soldering, hammering, embossing, trimming—to say nothing of the filigree work and granulation in the jewellery—required solving. Even more numerous were the problems peculiar to each specific type of metal-work—bronze vessels and weapons, articles in gold and silver, etc. It was not known where so many new forms originated and what influenced their development. Many of these forms were known from objects of undoubtedly Cretan origin found in the Mycenaean region of mainland Greece or the Greek islands.

Round the palaces were found the remains of cities that could not be fully explored. It was ascertained that other cities grew up round harbour installations, while certain settlements seem to have served various other purposes. As more discoveries were made, fresh problems were raised about the nature of these settlements, the sites chosen for them, and the general principles of their planning. Scholars wondered how many harbour installations were needed for shipping, and of what type. Had any large-scale public works been undertaken, and if so, how?

As more was discovered about the New Palace settlements, questions arose about such social, political and economic matters as social classes, the standard of living in each class, the place of woman in society, the political organization of the monarchy, the hierarchy of officials, the organization of the armed forces, the relations between the various kingdoms, the foundation of royal power, the relations between religion and the State, the foundations of the so-called "Minoan peace", the laws governing private property, barter, and the coinage, the organization of trade and the extent to which it was controlled by the king, the import of raw materials, etc.

Three scripts
The discovery of archives in the palaces and royal villas showed that government was organized on bureaucratic lines. The decipherment of these archives could clarify many historical and cultural questions, and scholars therefore concentrated—and still are concentrating—on the many problems they have raised. Why were three types of script used at one and the same time? How far had writing developed by then, and why did ideograms—whose use, one would have thought, went back to the first beginnings of writing—appear side by side with the syllabic writing of the texts? The precise character of the archives was not known, nor was it clear why they had been compiled on clay tablets. It was not known how they could be deciphered or even in what language they were written. When they were finally deciphered some of these problems were solved, but a host of new ones arose. Why were these archives compiled in Greek during the last phase of the palace period? Were the texts written in the two other scripts really in the Minoan language? It was not certain if these texts would in fact throw much light on Minoan civilization or, indeed, if the problems of the script could be solved. When, how, and why was Linear A changed to Linear B? The exact chronological relationship of the three scripts needed clarifying. It was thought that the clay tablets represented an annual budget, but what, in that case, had happened to the earlier archives? Scholars

wondered what other materials had been used for writing on, if there really had been a Minoan literature, and whether the hieroglyphic writing on the enigmatic disc of Phaestos was in fact a religious text.

Colonial expansion or the spread of a culture?
The spread of Minoan civilization during the new palace period and the consequences of that spread raised some very important problems. Shipping was obviously highly developed as could be seen from the harbour installations, the many pictures of the sea and ships, and the fact that raw materials were imported from distant regions; but it was not clear whether this amounted to mastery of the seas, even though Greek tradition was very definite on this point. The new ships were ocean-going and could certainly sail beyond the Mediterranean, but it is not proved that the Cretans had established ports of call in distant places, as Evans suggests. They did found trading posts and colonies—Greek tradition is quite definite on the extent of Minoan colonization—but it might be doubted whether they pursued a regular colonial policy on the lines of archaic Greece. If they did, the extent of their expansion and the nature of their settlements remains obscure. Were they originally trading posts in foreign territory, peaceful penetrations after the manner of the Phoenicians in return for the benefits of civilizations? Some scholars thought that the birth of Mycenaean civilization might itself have been due to large-scale colonization in the islands and in mainland Greece, while others believed that it might have been the result of Helladic invasions of Crete round 1600 B.C., at the end of the first New Palace period. What were the consequences of the colonial settlements in regions such as the islands of the Cyclades and the Sporades, the Peloponnese, Attica, Boeotia, the Dodecanese, Cyprus, Phoenicia, etc.? Phoenician civilization itself might have owed a great deal to the colonial settlements on its coasts. Some of the evidence suggested that not all the colonies were established for the purpose of settlement; some may have aimed at the exploitation of raw materials in regions that produced them, e. g., Melos, the Pontus, the Iberian Peninsula, the Lipari Islands, the Balearic Islands, etc.

The need to obtain raw materials in exchange for manufactured goods oriented Minoan trade towards the great centres of Egypt and the Near East. Evidence for this commercial penetration and for the setting up of trading posts had to be found. Records of it might also be discovered in the archives of the peoples concerned or in pictures showing imported manufactured products. This evidence required careful interpretation, for it might refer to entirely different contacts, such as diplomatic gifts or the payment of tariffs to secure trade agreements. Archaeologists discovered more evidence for trade relations with Egypt than with the rest of the Near East, but the colonial settlements on the Phoenician coast show that Phoenicia had very real links with Crete. The Cretan *Keftiu* was often depicted in Egypt, and this suggests that the Cretan settlers in the Near East had contacts with Egypt. Crete does not seem to have imported many objects of art from these countries—or at least few have been found during excavations, and these have been confined to a few categories, such as alabaster and other stone vases, scarabs from Egypt, and cylinder seals from the Near East. This rather puzzling fact raises the problem of mutual influences, especially in art.

At first, research was confined to central and eastern Crete since evidence for the spread of Minoan civilization to western Crete was not very encouraging. It seemed that western Crete had remained outside the sphere of Minoan civilization, at least during its periods of prosperity. This lack of evidence, however, might have been due to inadequate investigation. If, on the other hand, there really were no traces of the Minoans, western Crete must have contained some other civilization—perhaps the Cydonian civilization of the Homeric tradition—unless it remained uninhabited. Research would produce evidence to support one or other of these hypotheses. Some isolated remains later came to light, suggesting that western Crete had been far from adequately explored. It seemed certain, however, that it did not share in the rise of Minoan civilization to any appreciable extent, and the reasons for this had to be found.

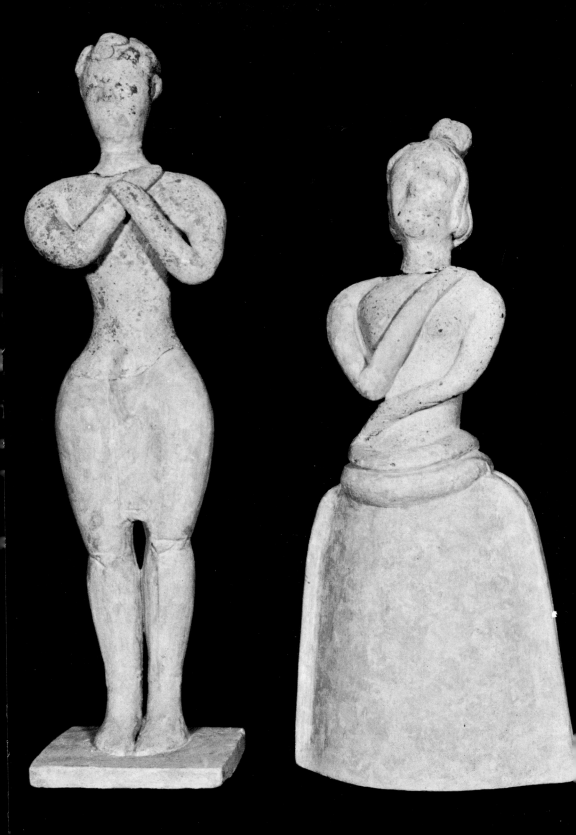

33

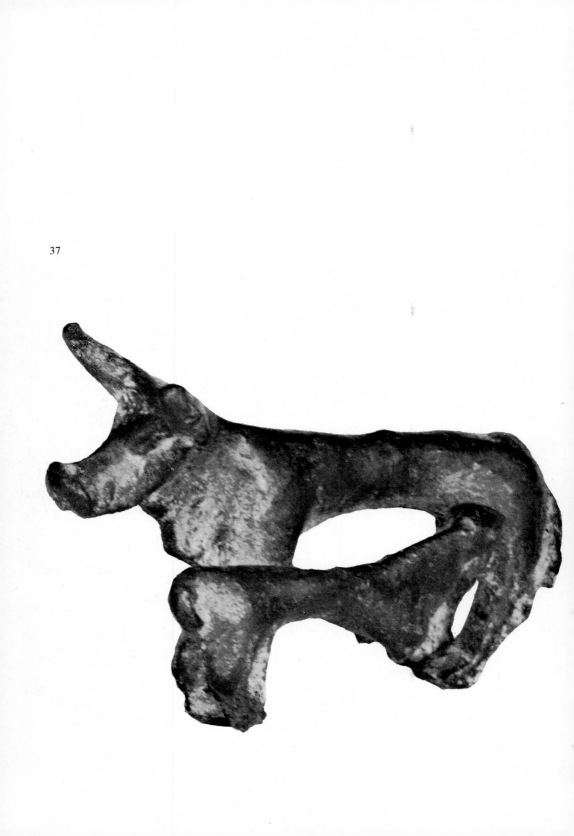

Beliefs

The evidence showed that religion developed along unchanging general lines and there was such a wealth of evidence that a very complete picture could have been formed of religious life in the New Palace period if it had not presented so many problems of interpretation. It was not clear whether the Minoan gods, who were personifications of nature, were really limited to a few figures, nor had the role played by these deities been defined. Did they personify nature in all its aspects or merely as a mother figure?

The places of worship were similar to those of earlier ages, but their organization remained obscure. It seemed puzzling that no temples had been built, even during the prosperous New Palace period. Scholars could not explain the disposition of the palace and domestic sanctuaries. Many of the earlier features of the form of worship had been faithfully preserved, but some innovations had been introduced and an established ritual was in process of evolution. A whole series of questions remained unanswered: what was the form and scope of consecration? What festivals were organized in honour of the gods and what was the part played in them by music, dancing and athletic displays? Were the Cretan bullgames connected with religious ceremonies? What was the part played by sacred animals, especially the bull? Were the special methods of catching bulls dictated by religious rules? What was the meaning of the sacred symbols in use? Was the worship of nature accompanied by ceremonies connected with germination, as in the cycle of the eastern religions? What was the role played by demons and supernatural beings such as the sphinx and the griffin? To what extent had ancient magic survived? How was the prieshood organized and was the royal family at its head? What were the vestments and insignia worn by the priests? The contents of the tablets might throw some light on Minoan religion and worship, but it was not certain how much.

The dead had to be given a home for their life in the next world, and this led to the construction of tombs in the form of complex underground chambers with separate vestibules and entrances—a development from the earlier type of tholos tomb. Much more information was needed about their evolution, the outside influences that might have led to it (especially the influence of mainland Greece), the way which individual necropoles were organized, the preservation of royal tombs and their consecration for the worship of dead kings, the evolution of burial rites, the objects that were buried with the dead, and finally the desecration and spoliation of the tombs.

That the new palaces and the Minoan cities suffered repeated and radical catastrophes was confirmed by the study of their remains. Little was known, however, about the causes, extent, and consequences of these disasters. Some scholars attributed them to invasions or internal dissensions and explained the growth of a mixed Creto-Greek civilization, the Mycenaean civilization, by the admixture of a foreign element of Greek racial stock. Others ascribed them to geological upheavals, particularly earthquakes. It was also uncertain how many catastrophes had occurred before the final destruction. It was thought that one of these catastrophes was caused by a volcanic eruption, and the attempt to verify this hypothesis raised fresh problems. It was not known how the most precious objects were carried off or pillaged after each catastrophe. One of the most controversial problems concerned the final destruction of the palace of Knossos. At first it was thought that it had been caused by the invasion of the Achaeans, though Evans maintained that it was due to geological factors. The decipherment of the tablets, however, revealed that the Achaeans had already been masters of Knossos for half a century. The catastrophe could have been due to an earthquake, but equally well to a rising of the oppressed native Minoans against the occupying power. It was also possible that the dating of the tablets was wrong—a mistake that could be due to a misunderstanding about the manner in which the archives at Knossos were discovered. This theory has recently been supported by the philologist Leonard Palmer.

The Post-Palace civilization

Minoans, Achaeans and Dorians

It has been established that despite the final destruction and disappearance of the palaces, Minoan civilization continued without any fundamental changes although at this time Mycenaean elements were beginning to appear. Mycenaean settlements became increasingly numerous. Scholars wondered therefore whether the palace at Knossos had ceased to be an administrative centre and whether—as Evans maintained—it had been only partially reoccupied. Palmer, on the other hand, supported the view that it survived in all its splendour until the Dorian invasion and that, until then, the Achaean kings had used it as a political centre with an organized life and regular archives. The extent of Achaean settlement in the island remained unknown and it was not clear how the Minoans became so completely assimilated that their civilization at the end seemed to be genuinely Mycenaean. What special features were due to Minoan survivals? Little was known about the evolution of civilization in Crete during this period and how it compared with other Mycenaean cultures, or about the relations of Mycenaean Crete with other Mycenaean centres and the great civilized countries in general. The population figures for the island were unknown, and it was a mystery how this the new civilization spread to western Crete. Was the Minoan religion changed as a result of the Achaean invasion? Did the information on religion obtained from the Creto-Mycenaean archives agree with the archaeological evidence, and was the appearance of the first independent temple buildings due to Achaean influence? Some peculiarities of Creto-Mycenaean religion, such as the wide-spread use of sizeable figurines with arms raised at right angles, remained to be explained. Burial customs in Crete at that time were very similar to those in the rest of Mycenaean Greece. But it was not certain whether some of the earlier customs, such as the use of sarcophagi and the belief in the apotheosis of the illustrious dead, had survived, and whether these coexisted with the newly introduced worship of heroes.

All the Mycenaean centres in Crete were suddenly destroyed, and by tradition this was attributed to the Dorian invasion. However, this event in itself raised many complex problems that have not yet been solved. The destruction of these centres coincided with the end of the second Mycenaean period; a third and final phase followed that marked the transition to the so-called proto-geometric civilization. This final period produced some important innovations: iron, cremation of the dead, garments fastened with buckles, geometric designs in the decoration of vases, and buildings placed on high acropoles. Were these introduced by the Dorians? If they were, the Dorian invasion must have been gradual and much earlier than was originally believed. There is also some uncertainly about the fate of the Minoan population. Were they driven into the mountains of eastern Crete? They probably settled in the sub-Minoan towns found in the Lassithi mountains and the Eteocretans—the "pure" Cretans—in eastern Crete were the last survivors of their race. We cannot be certain unless we can solve a number of other problems, especially that of the date when the Minoan civilization ended.

Survivals and memories
A brilliant civilization produced by such a dynamic people could not vanish without leaving any traces. It seemed unthinkable that everything Minoan and Achaean should have been obliterated. During the dark "middle ages" of the geometric period, some vestiges had assuredly survived as a latent force among the subjugated but still dynamic population. Scholars were confronted by an exceptionnally complex problem: they had to explain the origin of the "Greek miracle", that is the rebirth of the civilization in a new form. Two factors contributed to this: the old pre-Hellenic tradition and the new Hellenism. One of the basic problems is that of the major role played by Crete in this development.
Throughout the geometric "middle ages" the memory of past glories survived, no doubt confused and fragmentary and often shrouded in the mists

of myths and legends, but nevertheless based on an earlier historical truth. Echoes of this tradition are found here and there in Greek and Latin literature, in texts of great dissimilarity and of very unequal value. Valuable information could be gleaned from a close critical study of these texts. Of course, this fascinating subject raised new problems. What was the basis for the Homeric tradition concerning certain Cretan towns, the cave of Eileithyia, Minos and his brothers, and the five peoples of Crete? There was some doubt about the correct interpretation of the verse about King Minos:

'Εννέωρος βασίλευε Διὸς μεγάλου ὀαριστύς? [1]

The civilization of the Phaeaces in the Odyssey in many ways resembles the Minoan, but it was not certain whether it really had any connexion with it. The legend handed down by Plato of the submerging of Atlantis may be a reference to the history of Minoan Crete and its sudden destruction. The religious myths of the birth and upbringing of Cretan Zeus in the sacred caves of Ida and Diktys, and of the tomb purporting to be his, seemed to derive from ancient religious beliefs in the young god of vegetation. It was thought that the myths of the sacred marriages between bull-gods and queens and princesses like Europa or Pasiphae might go back to some of the beliefs of pre-Hellenic Crete. Legends associated the great sanctuaries of Eleusis, Delphi, Olympia and Delos with Crete, but it was not known whether there was any real basis for this. It was wondered whether the traditions of the Curetes, the Idaean Dactyls, the Telchines and the Cretan demons in general were an echo of the age when Minos ruled over the sacred island. Did Daedalus, with his amazing skills, personify the achievements of Cretan art, and was the tale of the Minotaur and the battles fought in the Labyrinth derived from a distant memory of the Cretan bullgames round the palace of Knossos? Again, the legendary expeditions of Minos to Megaris and Sicily might have had their origin in the political expansion and colonization

[1] "Minos ruled for nine years in friendly intercourse with Zeus".

of the New Palace period, while the mythical colonization of the islands by the followers of Rhadamanthus might have been a projection of similar designs of the Minoans in this direction. It was possible that the confrontation of the two rival powers of Attica and Crete in the Theseus legend corresponded to the actual confrontation of the Minoan and Achaean worlds, and that the traditions ascribing the foundation of Cretan towns to Achaean leaders or immigrants from Arcady originated in the Achaean occupation of the island.

These were only suppositions, and scholars were faced with the problem of confirming or refuting them. In this way, they hoped to explain how the memory of a long vanished civilization survived in Hellenic times and to elucidate many controversial points that could not be clarified by archaeological evidence alone.

II

The methods used for the exploration of prehistoric sites in Crete have been steadily improved and refined. The objectives are becoming more clearly defined and this combined with the tremendous advances of modern science, will undoubtedly lead to further progress. The earliest archaeologists made many mistakes and overlooked much of the vital evidence because they did not understand the fundamental problems of the civilization they had discovered and were preoccupied with the search for treasures and sensational finds. While modern scholars may severely condemn this attitude, they nevertheless recognize the great contribution their predecessors have made to Cretan archaeology. Below we shall deal briefly with methods used to define the aims of archaeological research, the classification of evidence, the prospecting of sites, the conduct of excavations, the preservation and restoration of finds, their dating, their publication, and their presentation on the site or in museums.

Written evidence and language

Criticism of the texts

As was to be expected, after the geometric "middle ages" which left no written documents, the evidence in Greek and Latin literature is poor, fragmentary, mixed with extraneous elements and mostly shrouded in myth. It is often difficult to decide whether the authors were referring to the prehistoric or proto-Hellenic period, for many of the towns they spoke of retained their pre-Hellenic names, e. g., Knossos, Phaestos, Lyktos, Lykastos, Amnisos, and Rhytion, all of which had been mentioned by Homer. Only by a thorough critical study could the historical facts be extricated from the traditional myths and religious legends. Scholars had to identify later modifications and accretions derived from other traditions and myths.

Study of place-names

The study of pre-Hellenic place-names mentioned by ancient geographers, travellers, and lexicographers or found in nomenclatures, inscriptions, or on Greek coins has been a valuable aid in locating prehistoric sites. Even before the great excavations had begun in Crete, linguists such as Kretschmer had recognized the pre-Hellenic names by their characteristic endings and forms, and they were subsequently studied by Fick and other scholars. Many such place-names have survived to this day, and the complete list which is being prepared by the Society of Cretan Historical Studies at Heracleion will be of great value. These names can be extremely helpful in tracing the sites of Minoan settlements, sanctuaries, etc. Lexicographers have done much to elucidate the meanings of certain pre-Hellenic words, whose roots frequently occur in place-names and in the names of deities. Thus "Za" in such names as Zakathos or Zakaros means "earth", while the name of the goddess Britomartis means "sweet virgin". It has also been shown that a number of general terms—names of animals, plants, trees, flowers, etc.— were derived from the pre-Hellenic vocabulary. Many pre-Hellenic words have been recognized in the Homeric epics.

Epigraphy

Although only a few written texts have been unearthed, it would be of inestimable help to archaeologists if they could be fully deciphered and interpreted. So far this has been possible only in the case of the clay tablets written in the so-called Linear B script which was an adaptation of the earlier Linear A. As the tablets in both these scripts seem to have been used for keeping accounts, there was not much hope that their decipherment would yield any important historical or literary information. There is even less hope of deciphering the earlier hieroglyphics which were used for short inscriptions on seals and on clay tablets of prismatic form. The hieroglyphs occur on the strange clay disc from Phaestos, and there perhaps they may represent a hymn to a god. So far no bilingual texts have been found that would help to decipher them, and they are not linked in any way with Egyptian or cuneiform writing. The only hope seems to lie in collating certain syllabic signs with those in the much later Cypriot script and in using the clues provided by the ideograms whose meaning is usually clear.

The system of numbers and measures was fairly easily deciphered by observing the units in each class and the manner of calculating; it appeared that numbers were based on decimals, the measures on the unit of twelve. The decipherment of the texts, however, was made more difficult by the fact that those who found them kept quiet about them for a long time in the hope that they would be able to decipher them on their own. Work on the scripts did not begin to bear fruit until after the publication of the texts found at Aghia Triada, Knossos, and Pylos.

The decipherment of Linear B
They were finally deciphered by an amateur, the English architect Michael Ventris, with the help of John Chadwick, the philologist. Ventris began with a long preparatory work, establishing statistics on the frequency of syllabic signs at the beginning, in the middle, or at the end of words, and on the changes of certain signs in combinations apparently composing the same words but in different cases or with the addition of suffixes or prefixes. The decipherment was based on the recurrence of three elements—the "triplets"—in given combinations, which had been noticed by an American scholar, Alice Kober. It was thought at first that the language would closely resemble Etruscan, but then it seemed that the language of the Linear B script might be Greek, in which case it had to be borne in mind that the orthography would cause certain difficulties of transcription. On this hypothesis a kind of grid was prepared and the syllabic signs arranged in vertical and horizontal columns according to the initial consonant of the syllable and the vowel that followed. This classification was made on the basis of the changes observed for the case or gender ending of the word,

without however determing the phonetic value of the syllabic signs. At the head of the columns of syllables with the same vowels were placed the signs which from their frequency appeared to represent the corresponding simple vowels.

The phonetic values were determined on the basis of the hypothetical but highly probable identity of certain words: *Amnisos, Knossos, Tylissos* (place-names); *Amnisios, Knossios, Tylissios* (describing the people); *Amnisondé, Knossonde, Tylissonde* (the "triplets", describing the places); helpful, too, were collective words used in additions, the words *Kouros* and *Kore* following the ideograms for man and woman, etc. On the basis of these hypothetical values, which were then applied to other words, it was possible to determine the values of other syllables, and these were placed in the grid.

The application of these values to the texts—checked against the ideograms —began to give positive results. Some minor errors in the initial classification in the grid were easily corrected. The two scholars then published the result of their research in their well-known article, "Evidence for Greek dialect in the Mycenaean archives" (1953) in which they explained their basic methods and gave the transcription and interpretation of a few texts from Knossos and Pylos. They admitted that, in order to interpret the texts as Greek, they had made use of a peculiar and highly simplified orthography and a very archaic idiom, resembling that of Homer.

The publication gave rise to a lengthy and keen discussion. It became clear that there were still serious objections to the decipherments, for the authors had not shown every step in their working, and the few texts they had translated seemed questionable since the orthography was so free that there were many different ways of reading one and the same word. Some of the ideograms agreed with the transcriptions, but then it might have been precisely those ideograms that had led to the interpretations of the script. But there was a strong swing in favour of Ventris' decipherment when the phonetic values were applied to hitherto unknown texts and the ideograms in these texts confirmed that the right method had been followed. The most important of these texts were: the "Tripod Tablet" from Pylos, in which the words describing tripods and vases with three or four or with no handles were illustrated by the corresponding ideograms; and the "Horse Tablet" from Knossos, in which the names of animals such as horses, foals, and donkeys could be verified from the accompanying ideograms. Some tablets showed that the transcription of such words as "breastplate" and "helmet" agreed with the ideograms for these terms, while others convincingly described aromatic plants and offerings to a number of Hellenic and pre-Hellenic gods. Gradually scholars withdrew their objections and—with a very few exceptions—accepted the decipherment unreservedly.

Although the basic validity of the decipherment was recognized there was naturally some disagreement about the rendering of the texts, which could be interpreted in a number of different ways, so that only hypothetical conclusions could be drawn from them. Moreover, the texts themselves consisted of accounts repeating the same stereotyped expression and containing many proper names, so that they could hardly throw much light on fundamental historical problems. Nevertheless, one highly important conclusion emerged—that Greek was the language used for administrative purposes in the final Palace Period at Knossos.

As Linear B was an adaptation of Linear A, the same phonetic values could clearly be applied to similar or analogous syllabic signs. This method was used and showed that the texts were written in an unknown language, probably Minoan. Unfortunately, there are extremely few texts and these often fragmentary, again consisting of accounts, so that nothing important can be deduced from them. Even the nature of their language is doubtful: Palmer thought it was the old Indo-European language of the Luvians of Asia Minor, while Cyrus Gordon claimed that it was a Semitic language. The name of the deity *Assassara* or *Assassarame* frequently appears on altar-offerings.

Prospecting archaeological sites

Evidence on the surface
As the written texts do not give any substantial help, the bulk of our knowledge must come from excavated remains.

Prehistoric sites may be located through simple observation. We know what kind of sites the Minoans generally chose for their settlements: low hills, points from which they could control passes, necks of small peninsulas flanked by bays, sheltered creeks, islets near the shore, picturesque sites at the confluence of rivers or close to a spring, etc. The remains of buildings are usually noticeable on the surface even if they are scattered and not easily identified: megalithic walls, scattered architectural elements, fragments of material from flooring or roofs, etc. Moreover, at such sites there are always numerous sherds spread over the ground and these can easily be recognized and dated even though they are fragmentary and worn. The hill settlements are typical and are known in Crete as *Kefalia*, *Kefales*, *Papoures*, and *Mouria*. They are very different from the Greek acropoles which were natural strongholds and inaccessible. Their mounds are due to the accumulation of material that piled up with the successive destruction of buildings and their soil—enriched by the centuries—has become fertile and is called "Greek" by the peasants. The sites of isolated settlements (farms, villas, frontier posts) usually control important roads or other key positions. Such sites show relatively few traces of remains. Typical, too, are the sanctuaries on high mountain peaks or on hills overlooking important centres; remains of buildings are rare on the whole, but it is easy to find fragments of clay offerings on the surrounding slopes.

Once the site of a settlement is known it is not difficult to find the necropoles. They were usually situated on the slopes of one of the surrounding hills, and with careful observation we can recognize the traces of ancient or recent disturbances from the faults or hollows in the soft rock. Tomb buildings, whether round or rectangular, often look like small mounds. Scattered over the ground are piles of potsherds, fragments of clay chests *(larnakes)*, or pieces of sepulchral urns *(pithoi)*. Similar remains are also found on sandy beaches near Minoan settlements for these were used for systematic burials, especially during the middle Minoan period. It is much more difficult to discover royal tombs for they were carefully hidden in isolated spots, often far from the palace centres. However, as they were monumental buildings we may sometimes find traces of them on the surface.

Detection by scientific methods
Today—thanks to the progress of science—more sophisticated methods can be used to detect archaeological sites. Aerial photography shows differences in vegetation and the relief of the ground wherever buildings are hidden under the earth; geophysical methods detect anomalies in the transmission of sound or the soil's resistance to electricity; periscopes probe underground for subterranean chambers and have been used with outstanding success in Italy where they revealed unpillaged Etruscan tombs. These methods have not been used in Crete, mainly because conditions in the island have been so exceptionally favourable that they have not been needed. Nevertheless, such allied methods as observation of the density of vegetation and sounding the soil by means of long probes and auscultation have been used for a long time.

Chance discoveries
Some of the most important discoveries are often due to chance finds in the course of ploughing, road works, building operations, or quarrying. Although such finds are often concealed and sold clandestinely, or—through negligence, ignorance, or fear—are not reported, they have in many cases led first to soundings and then to large-scale systematic excavations with

outstanding results. Chance discoveries are often followed by partial destruction by clandestine excavations, for there is a traffic in antique objects. The following typical examples of such finds are drawn from my own experience.

On Profitis Ilias Hill near Arkalokhori, badgers brought to light bronze objects—mainly double-headed axes and daggers—that had been concealed in a small cave, collapsed since Minoan times, in which minor excavations had been made in the first decade of this century. The village children enjoyed watching the green flames these bronze objects produced when thrown into the fire. Finally a quarrel about the ownership of a small golden axe brought the discovery to the ears of the Archaeological Service. The cave, in the meantime, had been systematically looted by the grown-ups, and several gold and silver objects, chiefly axes, mysteriously began to appear on the market. The Service kept a close watch and managed to track down the source of these objects, apprehend the traffickers, and recover most of the treasure. Systematic excavation subsequently brought to light an important collection of metal offerings.

A pig nosed a stone vase out of a rubbish dump—and this led to the discovery of the archaeological site at Amnisos with the Minoan Villa of the Fleur de Lys and the altar of Zeus Thenatus! The discovery of the sanctuary on top of Piskokefalo near Sitia was due to the chance find of clay figurines of women with artistic hairstyles and clothes and of unusual terracotta objects of the "horn rhyton" style which had first come to light twenty-five years previously but had not attracted the attention they deserved. The peasant who had found them was dead, but a search of his hillside field revealed similar objects and this led to the systematic excavation of the

The discovery of the palace of Zakro

As a typical example of the use of archaeological clues may be cited the recent discovery of the fourth Minoan palace—the only unpillaged one in the whole Creto-Mycenaean cycle—at Zakro in eastern Crete. A small-scale excavation of the region at the beginning of this century had brought to light isolated Minoan buildings, decorated pottery, interesting bronze tools, and deposits of clay seals which provided valuable information on Minoan religion. These discoveries suggested that the site had been an important port for the palace trade with Egypt and Anatolia. Three exquisitely-worked gold objects from this site had found their way into the Giamalakis collection shortly before the Second World War, although it was rumoured that they had in fact been found much earlier. Repeated reconnaissance of the site strengthened the conviction that a palace centre might be discovered there. Stout walls could be discerned on the slope opposite the hill where the first finds had been made; lower down the hill was the massive base of a column; a long bronze sword and a jar had been found in the strip of garden on the level ground between the two hills; when the land was ploughed a number of square blocks of tufa came to light. The stone had obviously been imported by sea to be used for a large building; the quality of the pottery of Zakro showed that it came from organized workshops—probably palace ones. These clues helped to determine the most likely site of the palace. A minute examination of the huge piles of stones from the ruined building revealed a strong corner built of large cut stones. Finally, trial digs on the spot where the jar had been found brought to light a group of store-rooms with their contents still in place. The site was now established. Systematic excavation was begun and revealed a vast palace with unique archaeological treasures.

Stratigraphy and dating

The nature of stratigraphic evidence

To give a complete picture of the development of the site, excavation in depth must proceed according to the stratigraphy and continue right down to virgin rock. Each level must be examined in turn, clearly distinguished and its elements photographed and described before destruction by the excavation continues. For later checking, samples are left either in the form of baulks or columns of undisturbed earth. In recent years a very careful stratigraphical examination has been made of the Neolithic levels under the central courtyard of the palace at Knossos. The most systematic stratigraphical research, however, has been conducted under the direction of Doro Levi in order to study the successive phases of the earlier palaces at Phaestos and the underlying Neolithic levels. The presence on the site of a great deal of pottery was extremely helpful.

The levels must be studied with minute care for they are not equally thick, nor are they always horizontal or continuous. They may have been disturbed in places by the later digging of deep foundations, cellars or wells. The old method of excavating by metre or half-metre and taking out the pottery has now been abandoned. But if the demarcations between the levels are not noticed in time—and they are not easily distinguished in the absence of sterile levels, levels of destruction, fire levels or accumulations of rubble—grave mistakes may be made. Moreover, deep trenching, levelling, or other operations may have brought very old levels to the surface or, conversely, deepened more recent levels. Nevertheless, the experience gained in observing successive archaeological layers, their principal characteristics, and the objects—especially the pottery— they contain, has now made it possible to identify them even where they are irregular or disturbed and to evolve precise methods of dating.

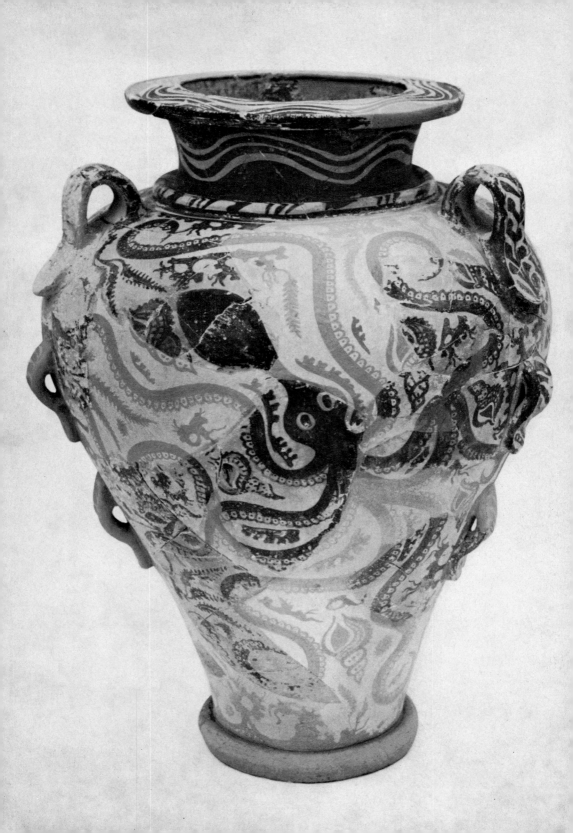

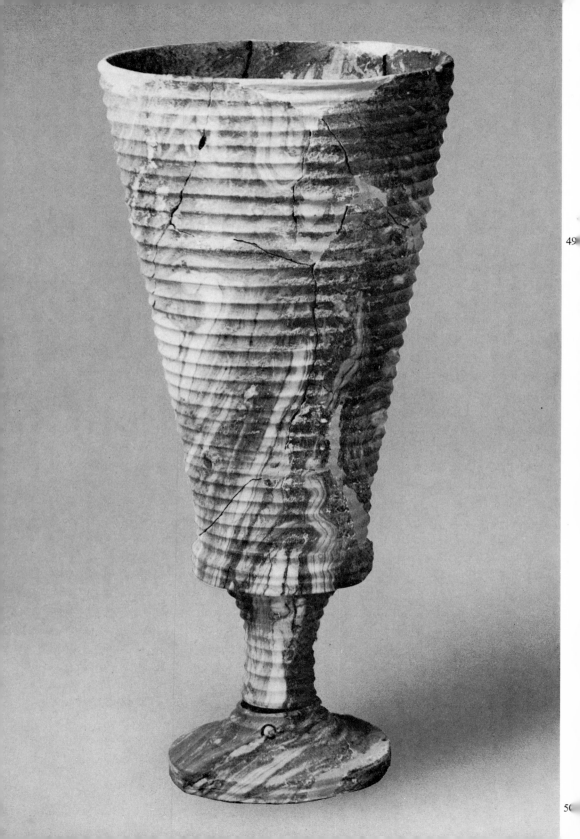

53, 54, 55 →

56

57

Stratigraphical research has helped to establish a comparative chronology. The study of pottery styles and types may sometimes fill the gaps left by the stratigraphical method of dating a pottery series. The decoration of vases, the evolution of their forms, and changes in pottery techniques followed a certain steady line of development that can be discerned from a close study of individual items. Of course, we must not forget that many old forms remained in common use even when new ones had been evolved; that there were times of retrogression and the speed of progress could vary according to the region; that the quality of palace products was much higher than that of ordinary everyday products and that mass production led to a great improvement in techniques but also to a deterioration in decoration and form. If the conclusions based on pottery styles and types agree with those obtained by stratigraphical methods they may on the whole be considered as reliable.

Various systems of relative chronology
The methods we have just discussed have been used to establish a so-called relative chronology dividing the whole development of Minoan civilization into ages, periods and sub-periods. The first system to be adopted was that proposed by Evans in 1904; it was retained for a long time because of the great reputation of its author although it provoked strong criticism and although other systems had been proposed in the meantime. Evans, using pottery as a criterion, divided Minoan civilization into three main periods: the Early Minoan period, represented by the Sub-Neolithic or transitional styles found chiefly in eastern Crete and in the Messara plain; the Middle Period, characterized by the Kamares-style pottery with polychrome decoration on a dark ground; and the Late Minoan period, with its naturalistic styles later modified by Mycenaean influence. Each of these periods was in turn divided into three sub-periods, and each of the latter into two phases. This division into three and then nine was probably influenced by the general idea of a cycle of "birth–prosperity–decline" and by the tradition of the "nine-year reign" of Minos. Evans' division had two great disadvan-

tages: it did not take into account the successive catastrophes that formed the basic historical divisions, and it was based on insufficient stratigraphical data drawn from different parts of Minoan Crete. Stratigraphical research has been undertaken to check the validity of Evans' chronology, but the results are still under discussion.

Some scholars thought that the divisions should be based on bronze, the principal metal, and distinguished a Chalcolithic, a Copper, and an Early and Late Bronze Age. This system has obvious drawbacks because we know so little about the development of metal-working. Finally, the present writer proposed a chronology based on the principal catastrophes in conjunction with the history of the palaces which were the main centres of the civilization. This system has as its main periods the Pre-Palace, Old Palace, New Palace, and Post-Palace periods, each of which is subdivided into three phases separated by catastrophes.

A corresponding succession of periods has been observed in the neighbouring Mediterranean civilizations—Trojan, Cycladic and Helladic—and the comparative study of pottery and of trade has laid the foundations for a "comparative relative chronology".

Absolute chronology
An absolute chronology had to be established in order to determine the place in history of the Minoan civilization. But there were no written documents, no lists of kings, no astronomical information that could be related to known events, such as were available for other great civilizations of the time. The Parian Chronicle and the Chronology of Eratosthenes, derived from mythological genealogies, provide meagre information on the events of the final Minoan period: according to the former, Minos I reigned from 1462–1423 and Minos II *ca*. 1294; Idomeneus took part in the Trojan War in 1218–1209 according to the same chronicle, but in 1193–1184 according to the Chronology of Eratosthenes. Obviously, all these dates must be regarded with caution. It seemed possible, however, that, despite all the

difficulties, an absolute chronology could be established on the basis of Minoan objects and records of Minoans from Egyptian, Anatolian, Mesopotamian or even Indian sources, such as monuments or archives, for which the dates were known; and also from objects of known dates (from the latter cultures) found in clearly defined Minoan levels.

This method of double checking has yielded positive results in practice. Of course, any shortening of the Egyptian or the other chronologies involved a corresponding shortening of Minoan chronology, and hence of the chronology of other Mediterranean cultures and indeed of the chronology of the whole of prehistoric Europe. Some discoveries have been a great help in fixing definitive dates, such as the vases and fragments of vases found at Abydos, Kahun, and Illahun, the post-palace Minoan vases from the beginning of the third phase found at Tel el Amarna, representations of *Keftiu* in the tombs of eminent men of the 18th dynasty, mentions of *Keftiu* in Egyptian inscriptions and papyri and of objects manufactured by Cretan craftsmen on the tablets from Mari on the central Euphrates. Definitive dates could also be established from the discovery of an inscribed diorite figurine and the lid of a box *(pyxis)* belonging to King Khyan; from an alabaster vase with an inscription dating from the reign of Tuthmosis III found in a tomb in the port of Knossos, and from many other vases, scarabs, and cylinder seals found in Minoan levels. The absolute chronology of the earliest periods is still obscure. On the other hand, the chronology of the final Minoan period can be fixed with the greatest precision thanks to the Minoan settlements in the Phoenician and Philistine regions and to the close links between Crete and Cyprus and Rhodes.

The Carbon 14 method and dating by scientific methods
In recent years attempts have been made to establish an absolute chronology by methods drawn from physics, especially by the radiocarbon technique and the application of the thermo-remnant magnetism theory. The "C 14" method consists of measuring the radioactive carbon 14 content of

plants and other organic matter on the grounds that the original radio-active carbon 14 content is reduced by a half over a period of 5360 years. But this method is tricky and cannot take into account all the factors that may have acted on the material, furthermore the results may show a margin of error of 150 to 200 years. The findings obtained by the Carbon 14 method in Minoan archaeology have so far not been satisfactory since they are completely at variance with the absolute chronologies established by other methods. Thus, according to the carbon 14 method, the Minoan settlement of Thera was buried by lava *ca*. 1250 B.C., whereas according to other evidence this event took place some 300 years earlier. Again, the destruction of the Minoan palace at Zakro, which appears to have happened about 1450 B.C. would seem from the carbon 14 findings to have occurred at least 250 years later. It would appear that the calculations are falsified by unknown factors, and that these errors cannot be corrected until the method has been absolutely perfected. Methods based on the thermo-remnant magnetism theory have proved even more unreliable and have produced no valid results.

The Excavation

Organizing the work

The organization of an excavation will depend largely on its character, its aims, and the nature of the site. The archaeologist in charge of the excavation, who is known as the director, selects a team of experienced scholars and scientific advisers, architects and specialized technicians, photographers, overseers, foremen, and trained workers, and recruits such local workers as may be needed. From the start, the housing, feeding and water supply for all these people must be organized, as well as their places of work and even their leisure. The equipment requires careful attention.

Before the excavation can begin, questions of land purchase or expropriation must be settled or, in the case of trial digs, the owner's consent must be obtained. The excavated soil should be dumped some distance away, on a site that does not itself contain any ancient remains. Piles of stones on the surface are removed after being examined to see if they contain useful material, and the soil overburden is sometimes removed. The director explains the working programme to his team, gives general instructions, and assigns each member to his task.

Diaries, sketches and photography
The members of the team are usually responsible for their own sectors, under the general supervision of the director. The director supervises the work as a whole and keeps a diary on the basis of the daily reports of the excavators who make detailed notes of all they discover, even if it seems unimportant at the time. To these are added rough plans and sketches indicating the position of the main finds, both in plan and section, and drawings of all the objects that have been dug up. Lists of finds are made from the start and are constantly kept up to date; they show the numbers by which the objects are designated on the sketch or plan and under which they are inventoried. First impressions and ideas are also noted in the diaries and these may later be rectified, but without erasing or changing anything in the original entry. In the general diary, which is written up daily, the director puts down his own observations from the notes he has taken during the day's work. He is not only in charge of the whole excavation, but also deals personally with every difficulty that arises. He himself sometimes excavates tricky spots and is responsible for the accurate execution of the work.

The architect draws general and detailed plans under the immediate guidance of the responsible excavator, with constant reference to the sketches in the diaries. Everything is checked on the spot, and the plans are improved and rectified if necessary before definitive plans are made from them. An expert draughtsman makes drawings of groups of objects in the place where they were found, sketches the stratigraphic levels and everything noteworthy that might not show adequately on photographs.

The site is photographed before work starts, and every subsequent phase of the excavation is photographed with a series of different cameras. Groups of objects or noteworthy isolated objects are carefully cleaned and photographed *in situ*. In each case, several pictures are taken, for it would be an irreparable loss if there was only one and it was damaged or spoilt. Photographs are taken in black-and-white and in colour, the latter for projection and publication. Finally, the site is taken from every angle so that a complete overall record is obtained. Photographs are taken with wide-angle and telescopic lenses, with flash, from heights, etc.

The practical problems
The excavator must always remember that each phase in the excavation yields valuable information which must be fully noted before it is destroyed for ever in the progress of the work. Often, however, the circumstances make it necessary to speed up the work, and in that case the excavator must do all he can to record as much as possible. He must compile his reports objectively, omitting all speculation and supposition. The director of the excavation must be able to deal with difficult and unforeseen circumstances, for on his experience and judgment depends the timely recognition of important discoveries which may otherwise be lost. The preservation of remains may sometimes call for on-the-spot inspiration, but there are competent experts who can immediately apply appropriate methods to save or protect finds.

In the case of groups of buildings or very large buildings, their extent is determined by trial digs and by clearing the peripheral walls. The ground is divided into squares forming a "grid" so that the position and depth of the objects found may be noted. When the position of rooms has been roughly established in relation to the peripheral walls, their exact individual size is determined and a number is assigned to each. Excavation proceeds slowly and with extreme care once well-defined archaeological levels are reached. As soon as an object is found, it is cleaned with small tools and brushes by special workers or technicians. Groups of objects are never taken to the surface until they have been fully drawn and photographed. Objects found on the floor of an ancient building are treated with special care and wherever possible are left in place until the room has been cleaned and can be seen as a whole. This is not always easy—in fact, it may be quite impossible where objects are buried under the debris from the floors above. In that case, each layer is cleaned and photographed in turn. When too much rubble from upper storeys has accumulated, excavation is particularly difficult. Where buildings have been destroyed by fire the stones are reduced to lime and the wooden beams and supports burnt to ashes with the result that the architectural elements above them have collapsed. Partitions made from unbaked bricks decay, and fire turns the soil russet. Fire, on the other hand, also helps to preserve some materials by baking them—in fact, the Minoan tablets were saved in this way. Moreover, the shape of some architectural elements, e. g., columns, beams and pilasters, is preserved by carbonization. Where wood has rotted, its presence can be discerned in the darker colouring of the soil. The shape of a missing element can often be restored by pouring plaster into cavities left by rotted wood. Sometimes wooden objects have been perfectly preserved in underground pools of stagnant water, and in airtight clay.

The removal of finds requires special skill and experience. It is fairly easy to collect pieces of pottery, and these are usually sorted on the spot to facilitate their restoration in the workshop. But some delicate materials, such as bronze and silver, disintegrated stones and ivory, faience and glass deposits are much more difficult to remove. The removal of frescoed plaster presents great difficulties; it has to be taken off strip by strip on plaster splints and sometimes must first be glued to a fine cloth. Perishable materials like wood, woven rushes or cloth were preserved only in special circumstances in the damp climate of Crete; sometimes they are partially saved through being in immediate contact with metal or submerged in an underground pool of stagnant water.

Excavation of caves and tombs

The excavation of isolated tombs or of necropoles calls for a different kind of preparation and technique. Chamber tombs cut out of the rock and often situated several yards below the ground are located by observations of the surface or by trial trenches dug down to the virgin rock. The trenches may encounter "dromoi"—corridors cut out of the rock to give access to the tombs—or cavities caused by a collapsed ceiling. Special equipment for lighting and air supply is needed for the exploration of deep-lying chambers. The tombs are cleared with great caution so that all evidence of the manner of burial, cenotaphs, funerary rites, and the worship of the dead may be studied. Research is easier if the chamber has remained hermetically closed and there has been no fall of earth, but the walls and roofs may be in ruins and require special support. Besides the objects buried with the dead, the best preserved skeletons are also removed in the position in which they were found in the *larnakes* (chest sarcophagi) or *pithoi* (sepulchral jars). Sometimes a part of the tomb has to be removed together with the skeletons, or the tombs may be dismantled section by section and then reassembled. Great skill and care is needed in the removal of wooden sarcophagi which have decomposed. Nevertheless it has been possible in Crete—thanks to the progress of modern techniques—to remove undamaged from its narrow tomb a crumbling *larnax* with a skeleton inside. The sepulchral chest sarcophagus was then repaired in the workshop without extracting or damaging the remains it contained.

62

← 58, 59, 60, 61

63

64

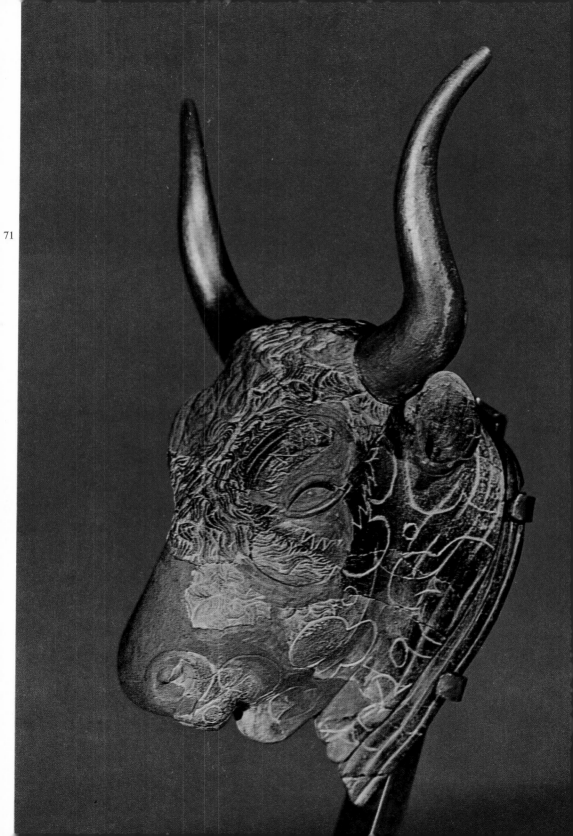

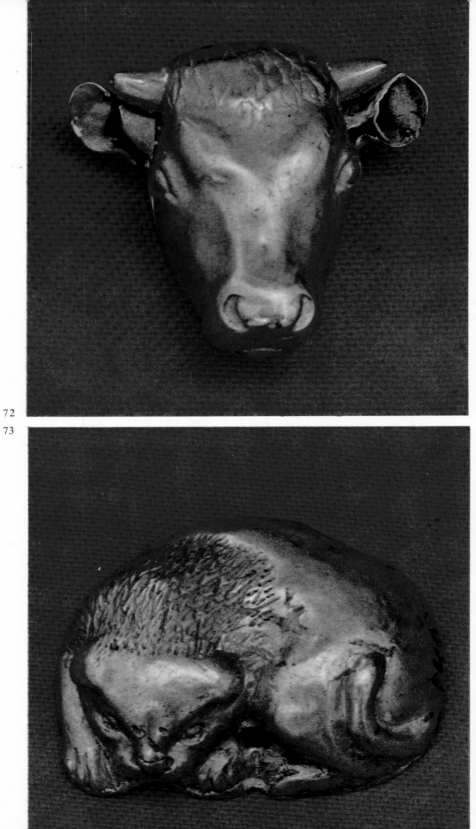

72

73

Underwater investigation

Underwater research and the exploration of caves raise additional problems. The latter poses problems of lighting, air supply, support, the investigation of levels encrusted with stalactites and mineral deposits, the removal of fallen material, etc. For underwater research a trained scientific and technical team is needed and special equipment for drawing, photography, etc. In Crete such research has not been undertaken on any large scale owing to a lack of means and of experienced, trained teams. It has been confined to locating and exploring sites close to the shore where harbour installations or the remains of sunken ships have been observed. Large areas where towns were submerged by land subsidence have been detected but not yet investigated.

The restoration of remains

Strengthening, protecting and restoring finds

Many remains that are dug up are of fragile materials and might disintegrate rapidly if provisional measures were not taken on the spot to strengthen and preserve them. Later on, more radical methods are used in the workshop. All repair work aims at making ruins more comprehensible by restoring much of their original form.

The fact that the walls in Minoan buildings were made of unbaked bricks contributes to their swift disintegration. The walls must therefore be strengthened internally with concrete which is then pointed with a material reproducing the colour of clay. They must be plastered and so must cracked or corroded floors of gypsum, limestone, or schist. A special support is placed beneath them to protect them from plants or roots that might damage them. The use of chemical products to suppress all harmful vegetation is one of the main measures of protection. However, the preservation of gypsum which is quickly worn away by water or friction still remains an unsolved problem. The only effective way to protect Minoan ruins is to put a roof over them, but opinions differ as to how this should be done.

Evans combined re-roofing with restoration, and undertook large-scale reconstructions of the buildings concerned. As his reconstructions were mostly conjectural and as he used unaesthetic materials and colours, his methods were severely criticized. The French excavator built saddle roofs, but this completely disfigured the sites. Finally the Greek Archaeological Service and the Italian School of Archaeology encouraged the use of transparent plastic coverings supported by thin metal poles, and this is now accepted as the best provisional solution.

Special circumstances may make it necessary to carry out extensive restorations, especially the replacement of architectural features or the completion of walls, staircases, tiled floors, etc. Where sections of floors on upper storeys have been found in place but subsiding, they have had to be re-levelled and supported. Where wooden beams had rotted and there was a danger of subsidence or collapse, they have had to be replaced with more lasting materials. From the evidence of other remains and of surviving pictures or models it has been possible to restore pilasters, frames of doors and windows, and columns and their capitals with materials made to resemble wood.

The secrets of the laboratory
After the excavation stage, finds are restored in the workshop. Clay vases or their sherds are cleaned by mechanical and chemical methods, and particular care is taken when, like the Kamares vases, they are decorated with fragile colours, or when they are made of a delicate clay. The fragments are then assembled and glued together with shellac or plastic cement, missing pieces being replaced by plaster. Metal reinforcement is used for very large vessels, for vases that have been distorted by great heat, and for vases that are badly chipped or of which only a thin outer layer has survived. Great care is needed in the cleaning and reassembling of stone vases for they are damaged by acids, and ordinary glues cannot always be used. The crystal rhyton from Zakro was reconstituted from 350 fragments, but the joins are hardly noticeable. Difficulties arise, too, from the flaking of

ivory objects and the disintegration of faience. Today we have special chemical products that help to harden and protect the surfaces, and coloured paraffin wax and plastic materials are used in conjunction with them. Missing parts that have been remade are coloured for aesthetic reasons on the principle of "moderate supplementation". Decorative designs are completed only if their pattern is definitely known.

The restoration of metal objects is more difficult, especially where the metal has undergone chemical changes. They are difficult to clean, and corrosion—especially of bronze—raises a formidable problem. Recently restoration has been tried by chemical conversion and by the use of special products for preserving the surface. Progress has also been made in the reassembly of broken metal objects.

The most striking advance, however, has been in the restoration of the Minoan frescoes. The old methods had serious disadvantages. They consisted of packing the pieces in plaster and strengthening them through internal plastering; quickly fading protective varnishes were applied, missing sections were painted in excessively bright colours, and heavy frames were used. Today varnishes are not used at all; the frescoes are cleaned by harmless mechanical and chemical methods; the fragments are fixed without being immobilized; care is taken to preserve the impression of a mural painting by the use of very light supporting frames, and retouching is done in discreet colours, no more being added to the picture than is necessary for an understanding of the subject. The whole is then protected by thin transparent sheets of plastic. If the fresco is too badly damaged, no attempt is made to restore the whole composition, and the fragments are exhibited as they are, together with explanatory sketches of the subject. Some frescoes which had been incorrectly reconstituted have now been re-done more convincingly, and several new fragments have been added which could not be fitted in previously. Thus the "Young Crocus-Gatherer" has now been changed into the "Apes Gathering Crocuses" and the "Holy Communion" has become the fresco of the "Libation Ceremony".

The study of materials and techniques
The materials used by the Minoans are studied on the site as soon as the first buildings and objects are discovered, and their examination is then continued in the laboratory by archaeologists, architects, and technicians. The nature of the materials, their provenance, and the ways in which they were used is investigated. Thus excavation adds to our knowledge of architecture and building, of the technique of making stone vases (especially revealing are the half-finished ones), of raw materials and tools, of the techniques used for frescoes and pottery, and of metal working. Some processes are still unknown, and not until quite recently has it been possible to reproduce the black gloss found on the vases from Kamares and the fine granulation of Minoan jewellery.

All the physical sciences have been called to the aid of archaeology: geophysics, petrology and mineralogy, atomic physics, geology and palaeontology, botany and zoology, anthropology and human geography.

Exhibiting the finds

The Museum of Heracleion
All the objects discovered during excavations or by chance are exhibited in Cretan museums or collections, especially in the Museum of Heracleion which is unique of its kind. While the exhibitions adhere to the general rules of museum display, they also take into account the individual character of the object shown. The Museum of Heracleion was reorganized a few years after the Second World War. The new layout aims at giving a complete picture of the civilization from earliest time by grouping together objects that are representative of each age and period. The attractive display of objects in special showcases, in a set order, enables the visitor to follow

without effort the various aspects of Minoan civilization and to distinguish the most important items. The frescoes are shown in separate well-lit rooms. The recently acquired Giamalakis collection of Minoan objects, which is unique of its kind, is also exhibited separately. Many pictures, photographs, reconstructions, plans, and models help the visitor to gain a broad under-standing of the subject. The Scientific Collections are especially valuable to scholars, for the objects are grouped together just as they were found. There is a section on anthropology. Finally, the third and largest section of the Museum consists of well-catalogued store-rooms where the rest of the material from the various excavations is methodically assembled and easily accessible to scholars. One part is reserved for recently discovered objects awaiting exhibition.

This chapter only gives a brief outline of the methods used in Minoan archaeology from the detection of the site to the putting on display of the remains of one of the greatest and oldest of civilizations. In practice, they are more complex and difficult, and they are constantly being improved and refined.

THE RESULTS

III

Archaeological research in Crete has shown that the Mycenaean civilization, despite its original features, was undoubtedly derived from the Minoan. The development of the Minoans themselves could be followed from the neolithic age to the time when—as if by magic—the Helladic civilization appeared in a new guise of obviously Minoan origin. From then on the Cretan and Mycenaean cultures developed side by side, each following its own path. It was no longer necessary to look for the origin of the Mycenaean civilization outside Crete, although it had some features in common with that of such countries as Phoenicia.

The great newly discovered civilization was named after the legendary King Minos, the ruler of its most important centre, Knossos, although many other centres—especially in eastern and central Crete—must have contributed to its growth.

Pre-Palace Crete

The dawn of the civilization

It has now been proved that the Minoans were preceded on the island by a Neolithic civilization which underwent a long and slow development. Its long duration is proved by the depth of the levels of its settlements—the Neolithic levels at Knossos are the deepest in Europe—by the number of successive settlements, and also by certain links with the earliest phases of the civilizations of pre-dynastic Egypt, the Near East, and Anatolia. The excavations undertaken by Sir Arthur Evans—and later (1958–1960) by John Evans—at Knossos have thrown a great deal of light on the Cretan Neolithic Age, that is between 6000 and 2600 B.C. according to the Carbon 14 method of dating. It seems that the first settlement was simply an encampment. Soon, however, life became organized in a less primitive manner. The pottery produced was properly burnished and of a fairly good quality and often had a stippled decoration or small dots in relief. The custom of burying children beneath the floor of houses was gradually abandoned. Houses ceased to be mere huts. Dried brick or mud walls were built on stone foundations, and houses had several rooms and hearths and were properly planned. From the time of the Early Neolithic II there was little change in the manner of building. In the pottery, however, there was a progressive improvement in the shape of vases (mostly simple receptacles for domestic use), and with "ripple ware" a geometrical form of decoration came into regular use; finally, in the Late Neolithic Age, new effects were achieved by exposing the surface irregularly to firing, while in the final period fragile splashes of colour were applied—red, ochre and white—such as are found at Phaestos. Some primitive clay figurines and a few of the better-made stone ones may represent a goddess of fertility.

Towards the middle of the third millennium B.C. a sudden change occurred in Cretan civilization. A new, highly-developed culture appeared, with a new spirit; its swift rate of evolution was due to the introduction of new basic materials, especially metal. How can this be explained? Some think that the Neolithic civilization made a sudden leap forward as a result of the new techniques introduced from the outside, and that this coincided with a relatively small influx of a new racial group. Others claim that it was the new race from overseas that brought the new civilization and that the radical change in the culture of the island owed little to the survival of a considerable Neolithic element. Doro Levi denies that there ever was a proto-Minoan civilization and claims that the Neolithic, after the invasion by a new racial element, changed immediately into the Old Palace civilization to which it bequeathed the polychrome pottery in which it had made a little progress during its final phase. The new race certainly seems to have played an important role in the change to a new civilization which also reaped the fruits of the long Neolithic experience and of the influence

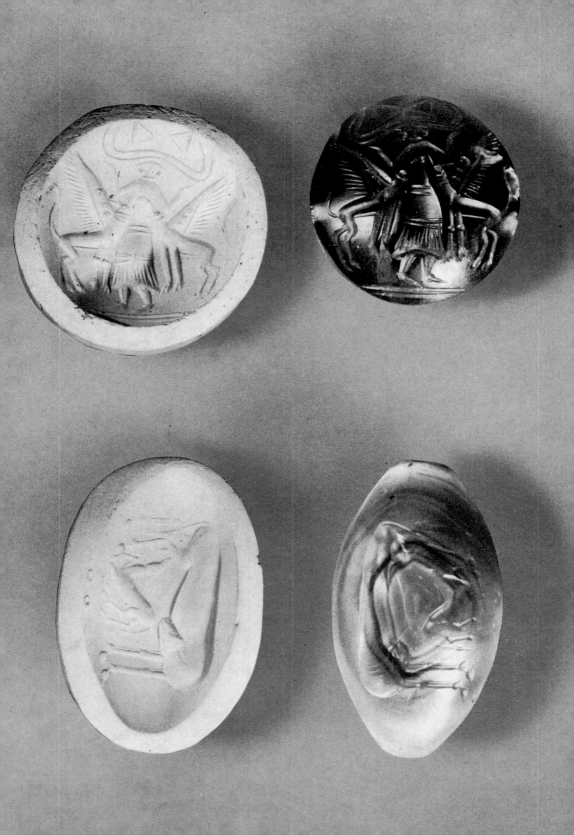

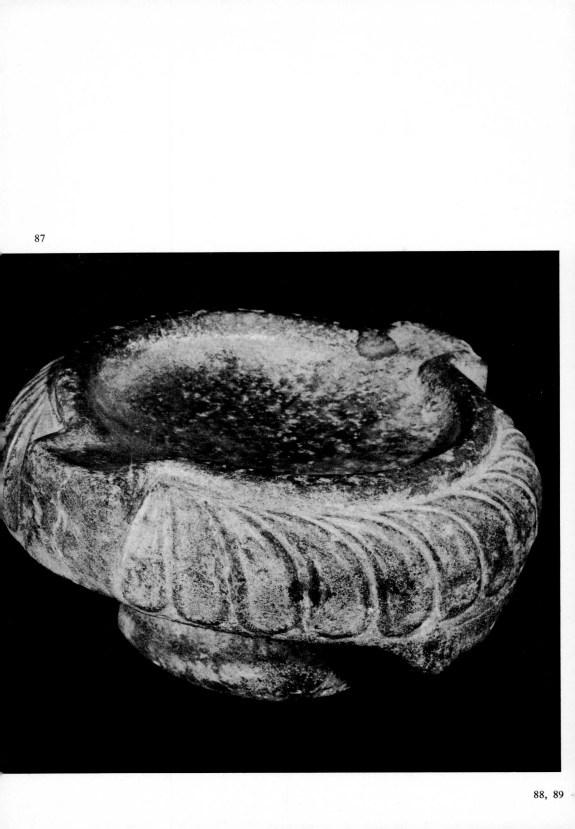

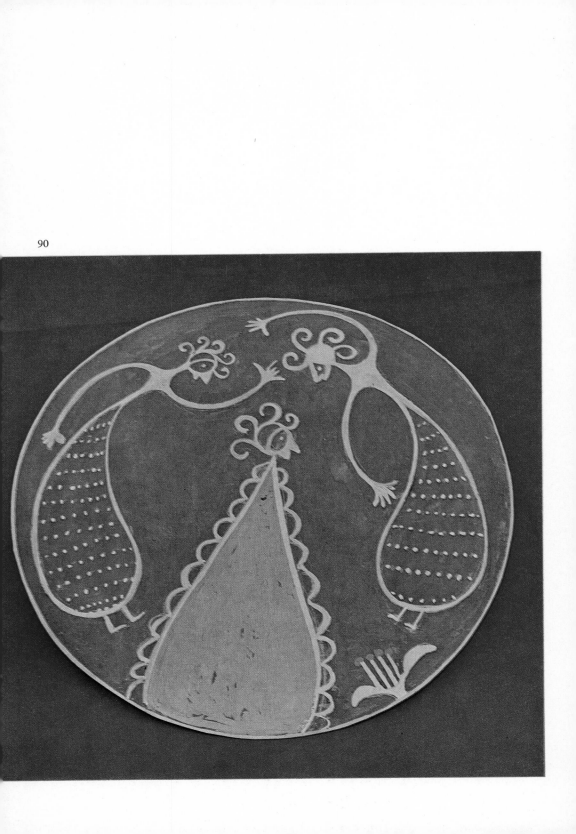

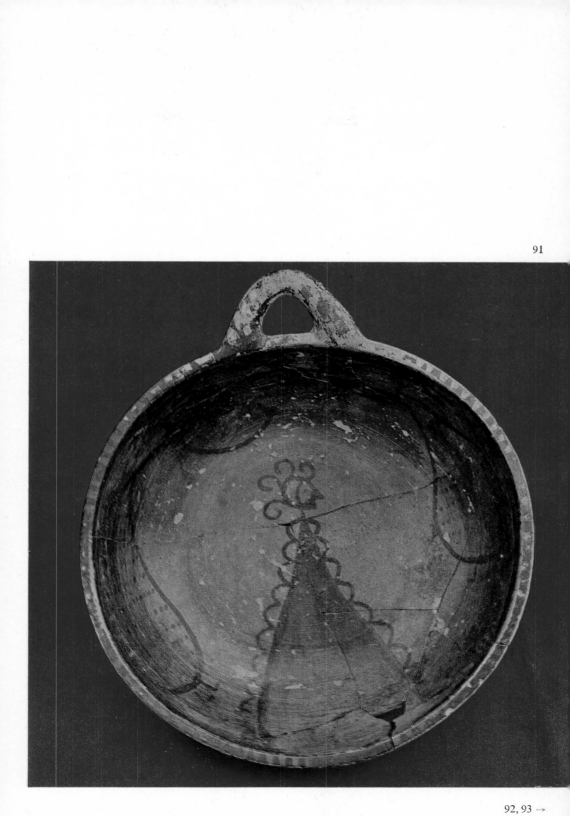

exerted by the surviving but unassimilated Neolithic elements. The geographical position of the island was exceptionally propitious and no doubt contributed to the tremendous progress made in all fields from that moment.

The evidence from a number of related studies—anthropological data, tools, general characteristics, distribution, etc.—has shown that the new racial group belonged to the "Mediterranean race" which from earliest times had spread through the whole eastern Mediterranean region—and later to the western Mediterranean—, establishing kindred civilizations with only local differences. The origin of the branch that settled in Crete has not been definitively determined. But it is clear that it had links with the proto-Libyan and Anatolian regions, and it is conceivable that the migrants came from both regions at the same time and that this resulted in the formation of a mixed racial type combining Libyan and Armenian anthropological characteristics. At all events, the newcomers were exceptionally energetic and active, driven by the need to survive to seek raw materials in distant regions and to supplement local resources by foreign trade. Thus they became an adventurous seafaring people.

The progress made during the Pre-Palace period
Systematic research over the last two decades has almost completely solved the problem of the Pre-Palace or Early Minoan civilization. It developed in three successive stages. The first period still retained a Sub-Neolithic character although it had a new energy and potentialities manifest even in its early pottery which it derived from the Neolithic tradition. This early pottery imitates the appearance of wood (Pyrgos style), of skin (Partira style) and of a basket-work (Aghios Onouphrios style). In the next two periods new styles were developed, using the oxidizing effect of fire (Vassilike style) and imitating the texture of metal (ribbing style) or the spiny shells of *Crustacea* ("barbotine" style). From the second period onwards, marked progress was made in architecture, gem- and seal-engraving and metal-working.

From this period, too, date the strong, many-roomed buildings of eastern Crete, the introduction of the spiral in pottery, the advance in bronze-working, the development of a sophisticated goldsmith's art, and the magnificent stone vases. Under the influence of Egypt, which even supplied some models, hard stones with a fine veined or mottled texture began to be fashioned into superb small vases in which the material was brilliantly adapted to the shape and function of the object. On some of these vases appeared the first carvings. The finest examples were found in the necro-poles of the small island of Mochlos (eastern Crete). Goldsmiths were producing elegant ornaments in which naturalistic designs were employed. The third and final period prepared the way for the first peak period, which began soon afterwards with the building of the first palaces. Large dwellings were built on the later sites of the palaces. The Cretan genius expressed itself particularly in engraving, and decorative and representational designs first appear in ivory and steatite seals of all sorts, but especially on cylinder seals. In pottery, decorations in light colours or white on a dark ground foreshadowed the polychrome style of Kamares. Stone vases began to be decorated with carvings and inlays. In metal-working the use of alloys had at last been mastered, and small, but strong, weapons and interesting vases could be produced. Goldsmiths introduced such innovations as filigree and granulation.

In tomb architecture, some outstanding forms derived from the simple hut and the circular enclosure were developed. Large circular stone tombs with corbel domes were used as common graves, and so were vast enclosures subdivided into numerous unroofed compartments where hundreds of dead were buried. These vaulted tombs—it has recently been proved that they were tholos tombs— are the oldest in Europe and later developed into the monumental Mycenean tombs.

We still know relatively little about the social, political, economic, religious, and private life of the period. The communal tombs suggest that society was organized on the basis of the *genos* (clan). What little we can conjecture about the way the Minoans lived is gleaned from the material remains of their civilization. One thing, however, is certain: they had already taken the first important steps in the direction in which their civilization would move, although its full development can be seen more clearly in the later periods. Relations with Egypt and the Near East had been strengthened, and the numerous Cycladic remains (figurines, clay and stone vases, daggers, etc.) found together with proto-Minoan objects show that there was a lively trade with the Aegean world. By this time Minoan civilization had acquired its general features and its special characteristics and these came to even fuller expression in its great peak period. A fine artistic sense, a delight in beauty, grace and movement, enjoyment of life and closeness to nature, these were the qualities that distinguished the Minoans from all the other great civilizations of their time.

Crete at the time of the Old Palaces

The foundation of the monarchies

It is difficult to say how power came to be concentrated in the hands of the kings and what led to the founding of the first palaces. It has been suggested that some of the local chiefs had been brought to the fore by internal dissensions. Some scholars think that the change was due to the arrival of new invaders—according to Palmer these were the Luvians, who were descended from a branch of the early Indo-Europeans and had recently settled in south-eastern Anatolia. This view seems to be supported by some place-names and other linguistic evidence and by a fairly close resemblance between the palace of Beycesultan and the earliest Cretan palaces. Nevertheless, it seems more likely that the Old Palace civilization is a direct continuation of the Pre-Palace one and that the new features in it had simply evolved out of the old. There are not enough points of resemblance between the Cretans and Luvians to support a theory of mass immigration. If, indeed, there had been any large-scale immigration it would have left traces of an early Indo-European type of language. The centralization of power probably arose from the need to counterbalance the organized powers of Egypt, the Middle East and Anatolia.

Architecture

The large old palaces have only been partially excavated because their ruins lie beneath those of the new palaces and are inextricably mixed up with them. Archaeologists believe that several of the principal features of the old palaces of Knossos and Phaestos were incorporated in the new palaces, and the excavators of the palace at Mallia were convinced that the main building of the old palace was adapted and used in the second one. However, there is no evidence for this. In any case, even if the old palaces were built on the same principles as the new ones, they differed from them in every other respects. This has been clearly illustrated by the excavations conducted by Doro Levi at Phaestos where the old palace buildings discovered at successive levels give a fairly good idea of their form and development. A complete group of storeyed buildings, attractively laid out and well adapted to the site and practical needs, were arranged round a vast rectangular central courtyard. Extensive levelling and artificial terraces in the hillside allowed the buildings to be spread over a wide area; they had magnificent raised façades overlooking the western courtyard and a whole network of connecting corridors and staircases. On the ground floor was a series of store-rooms and workshops, while larger and lighter rooms were used as living quarters, sanctuaries, etc. Thick wooden beams were built into the walls which gave slightly, and thus provided resistance to earthquakes. There were drains and dumping grounds. It has been shown that at Knossos the water supply was assured by terracotta pipes which carried the water for a distance of some ten miles.

144

The development of the palaces was accomplished in three phases with fairly extensive destructions between them. They can be followed through their successive architectural remains—especially clear are those from the new excavation at Phaestos—and through the study of pottery and more particularly the polychrome pottery of Kamares. Once the relative chronology of the three consecutive phases had been established it was possible, from comparisons with Egypt and the Near East, to fix the absolute chronology as 2000 to 1700 B.C. Evans thought that at Knossos the single palace developed from a series of independent islands of buildings round a space which later became the central courtyard, but this theory has no foundation in fact. The settlements surrounding the palace centres have been partially excavated, but not sufficiently to give us a clear idea of them. Crowded living conditions in serried multi-storeyed buildings set in squares seem to have been common. In the necropoles, domed tombs and funerary enclosures continued to be used, but most burials were in simple *pithoi* (jars) or very small sarcophagi which were buried in the hillsides or in the sand on the seashore.

Pottery

No art or industry of the old palace period is better known than that of pottery. Countless examples of great variety have been found at all levels, especially in the palace of Phaestos. The Kamares style—polychrome vases with decorations on a dark ground—is most varied and attractive. It had a wonderful harmony of shape and ornamental design. Each vase has a personality of its own. Although the basic decorative motifs were often repeated, they were combined in an unbelievable variety of ways, creating an almost kaleidoscopic impression. The subjects were often drawn from nature but they never lost their full decorative effect. Decoration in relief—grooved or barbed—was not uncommon on this pottery. These vases show amazing skill, not only in the expert handling of colour and the preparation of a polished metallic ground but in their perfect shape and the thinness of the fabric, which has been compared to eggshell. The best series come from the palaces of Knossos and Phaestos. In addition to this pottery which might be qualified as palace pottery, large quantities of simple utensils have been found, mainly practical things such as cooking equipment, pots, griddles, cheese-graters, cookers, funnels, sieves, charcoal-pans, lamps, coal scuttles, bellows, etc., all of them interesting and original. Although the potter's wheel was in general use at the time, hand-made vessels were not uncommon.

Other art forms

Clay modelling did not progress beyond the manufacture of simple votive objects for the sanctuaries. But many of these figures have a great deal of grace and spontaneity, such as the figurines of worshippers with their characteristic girdles and of worshipping women dressed in charming fashion with open bodices, high collars and artistic hairstyles, or the sculpted groups which include the first representations of bull games.

Unlike Kamares pottery, stone-cutting did not make any great strides and in this field no comparison is possible with the work of the Pre-Palace period. Nevertheless, there were some very fine stone vases, with inlays, engravings, incisions, and decorations in relief. The most interesting are the many votive vases or *kernoi* produced at the time.

Seal-engraving, on the other hand, made tremendous progress. Semi-precious stones were used as well as soft stones and ivory. Elegant seals, disc-shaped seals, and especially prismatic seals of all sizes, suitable for hieroglyphic inscriptions, were magnificently engraved with minute naturalistic designs. The royal seals, known from the imprints that have been preserved on clay, are of outstanding artistic value and have handed down to us portraits of kings and royal insignia. The inexhaustible variety of design is amply illustrated by the seals found in the palaces of Knossos and Phaestos. A seal work shop discovered near the palace at Mallia has thrown a great deal of light on the techniques used.

Life during the Old Palace period

Our picture of Minoan social, political, economic, religious and private life remains fragmentary. Society was no longer organized on the basis of the *genos*. Social classes were divided according to country and town property holdings, profession, or function in the centralized government. The government may have developed along theocratic lines, and each king ruled his own domain in close harmony and "peaceful coexistence" with the others. The development of writing led to the establishment of the first bureaucracy as is shown by a small number of tablets in Linear A found in the three palaces. The economy was not confined to agricultural production and industries supplying local needs but included an extensive trade, for the growth of shipping led to a wider distribution of goods. Relations with Egypt, Anatolia, and especially the Aegean world were strengthened, but there was no colonial expansion in the true sense of the word. There were only isolated settlements for the exploitation of raw materials (for example, of obsidian at Phylakopi on Melos) and perhaps a few trading posts.

Religion, as before, was founded on the worship of deified nature. Most of the evidence on it is sporadic and comes mainly from mountain sanctuaries, some sacred caves, and chapels in palaces or private houses; models that have survived help us to form a clearer idea of the sanctuaries, symbols, and sacred animals. We can also gather something about the rites and their purpose from numerous clay offerings.

Destruction and reconstruction

The final destruction of the old palaces was total and universal. Comparisons with data from Egypt and Mesopotamia show that it took place *ca.* 1700 B.C. Such total destruction could only have been caused by a geological upheaval, as there was no foreign invasion to account for it, and it has in fact been proved that violent earthquakes did occur at the time. Owing to the extent of the disaster, the new palaces were, from the start, built to new plans, either at a higher level on the same sites (the ruins were first banked up and covered, as at Phaestos, with a layer of broken tiles), or on completely different sites.

Palace architecture became markedly more monumental, with vast central and western courtyards, majestic façades and entrances, larger rooms, and probably more storeys. There were now hundreds of rooms laid out in even more intricate labyrinths. This form of the palace was retained until the end despite two intervening earthquakes as destructive as the first. Admittedly, there were alterations on the outside, and the interior decoration was renewed, but the appearance and general character of the whole remained unchanged. These are the palaces whose ruins have been discovered so far.

Radical reconstruction was accompanied by important progress in the arts, in technology and in relations with the outside world. The civilization enjoyed a second peak period and its achievements in every field were remarkable.

Crete at the time of the New Palaces

Originality of the Minoan civilization

Minoan civilization had acquired its definitive character. It was based on the close links between man and nature which were felt to resemble those between a child and its mother. Sensitivity was one of its predominant features. In art this was expressed in a feeling for grace, a love of movement and energy, and a taste for refinement and sumptuousness. The fear of death was almost obliterated by the ubiquitous joy of living. The whole of life was pervaded by an ardent faith in the goddess Nature, the source of all creation and harmony. This led to a love of peace, a horror of tyranny, and a respect for the law. Even among the ruling classes personal ambition seems to have been unknown; nowhere do we find the name of an author attached to a work of art nor a record of the deeds of a ruler. In this respect the Minoans differed widely from the peoples of Egypt and the Near East where exactly the opposite principles prevailed. The lively spirit of the

96

94, 95

Minoans was obviously sharpened and their imagination stimulated by their sea journeys, and the Mediterranean temperament contributed to their outstanding energy. The important part played by women is discernible in every sphere, and there is no doubt that women—or at least the influence of feminine sensitivity—made a notable contribution to Minoan art. On the whole, Minoan civilization bears a curious resemblance to Sino-Japanese civilization, although there was never any contact between the two. This is probably due to a similar attitude to nature.

This view of the Minoans is opposed by a Dutchman, Snijder, who holds the strange theory that they were "intuitive primitives" and that the splendid representations of nature in their art were produced in the manner of "intuitive" peoples or individuals who, in general, are backward, wholly devoid of creative intelligence and constructive thought, and incapable of reasoning or of deliberate adaptation. However, there seem to be absolutely no grounds for this supposition.

New Palace architecture

The detailed study of all the palaces so far discovered has proved that the new palaces were built to a predetermined architectural plan and were not the outcome of haphazard additions ("*Knospenagglomerat*", to quote a German archaeologist). The buildings were perfectly adapted to the space available, to the surrounding country, and to practical needs without detriment to the overall aesthetic effect. Both local and imported materials were used, all worked with meticulous care; gypsum and tufa pilasters and tiles, perfectly bonded, composed façades, walls, light-wells and courtyards. Partitions were decorated with plaster, with murals in many cases, and with marble facings. The floors were covered with gypsum, schist, or limestone slabs joined with mortar. The labyrinthine building contained many apartments laid out over several storeys, at unequal heights and arranged asymmetrically round a central courtyard; they were divided into sets, each with its own character and purpose, and linked by a number of corridors and staircases. There were splendidly decorated entrances and approaches on all sides, while the principal apartments were preceded by majestic propylaea. Long lines of store-rooms with connecting corridors contained provisions and rows of *pithoi* for the orderly safe-keeping of food reserves and treasures. A whole series of specially equipped rooms were kept for religious worship; there were sanctuaries with benches for idols, crypts with square pillars bearing carvings of sacred symbols, rooms for religious ceremonies, lustral basins, sacristies, treasuries, etc. The most typical example is the famous Throne Room in the palace at Knossos, with the lustral basin and the throne of alabastrine gypsum still standing undisturbed between the benches.

The royal apartments consisted of a suite of rooms with light-wells and surrounding porticos. Some were the king's apartments, some the queen's, and the smaller ones were probably for the princes. Vast halls with interior colonnades or rows of columns were used for audiences, receptions, banquets and council meetings. The kings had their private storerooms, distinct from those of the state and the sanctuary. The workshops have been identified by their special layout and also by the half-finished objects, the raw materials and tools that were found there. The domestic staff of the palace had their own quarters. The courtiers were lodged either in the palace or in attractive houses nearby. The recently discovered palace at Zakro, in a bay at the tip of eastern Crete, closely resembles the palaces of Knossos, Phaestos, and Mallia although it has some original features of its own. It was the only place that had not been pillaged before its discovery and contained a quantity of treasures.

Royal villas used as summer residence have been discovered in picturesque, cool places not far from the palaces; these were palaces on a small scale. Other villas and country houses have been found dotted through the countryside and fitted out with vats, olive-presses, kilns, etc. These may have been the residences of local governors or representatives of the king.

The Minoan towns, especially those near the large palaces, have not been adequately explored. However, we know some country towns, such as Gournia in eastern Crete, and parts of ports have survived, some on small roadsteads, e. g., Palaikastro and Zakro, and others on islets, and peninsulas such as Pseira and Mochlos. Here paved streets, level or stepped up the slopes, linked the groups of houses. We still know next to nothing about harbour installations, such as docks, beacons, slipways along the shore where small boats could be repaired or laid up, etc. All the urban centres had perfect drainage systems, sanitary installations, and domestic conveniences. There is no doubt that extensive public works—paid for out of the royal coffers—were undertaken in Minoan Crete. Although only a very few remains have so far been cleared, these have been revealing: viaducts, paved roads, look-out posts, roadside shelters, water pipes, fountains, reservoirs, etc. There is evidence of large-scale irrigation works with canals to carry and distribute the water.

The vicissitudes of the new palaces

As we have said, the development of the new palace centres was twice interrupted by great catastrophes, the first time round 1600 B.C. and the second time round 1450 B.C. The chronology of the intervening periods has been fixed with certainty on the basis of comparisons with Egypt and the Near East. The alabaster lid with the seal of the Hyksos pharaoh Khyan, the Egyptian alabaster vases found in the royal tomb of Isopata and in one of the tombs in the port of Knossos dating from the time of Tuthmosis III, the Egyptian scarabs and Syro-Hittite cylinders, the representations of the *Keftiu* in the tombs of prominent Egyptians of the 18th dynasty—all these enable us to fix the chronology of the New Palace civilization between 1700 and 1380 B.C. Its peak period began after the first catastrophic earthquake and lasted until the destruction of most of the palace centres caused, it seems, by the eruption of the volcano on the island of Thera *ca.* 1450 B.C. The final phase was more or less confined to Knossos where a new style of pottery, the Palace Style, appeared, obviously influenced by the new Mycenaean spirit. At first most archaeologists thought that this seemed highly unlikely; they believed that the other centres had also continued but had retained the old civilization unchanged. But the recent excavations at Zakro which have shown the close links existing between these centres and Knossos, have made this theory untenable. The Linear B tablets which constitute the palace archives of Knossos for the final New Palace phase have pro- that by this time the Achaeans were masters of Knossos. Therefore the final destruction of the palace could not have been due to the capture of the city by the Achaeans as was formerly believed. It seems equally unlikely that it was caused by a rebellion of the subjugated Minoans against their Achaean conquerors, for in that case it would have been followed by a new Minoan dynasty. For the time being, it seems most probable that Evans was right in supposing that the destruction was caused by a geological upheaval.

Tomb architecture

An extremely important fact has emerged from the most recent excavations, namely that the monumental tholos tombs, which were copied during the second New Palace period even in Mycenaean Greece, originated in the vaulted tomb structures of the Pre-Palace and Old Palace periods. All the intermediate links—e. g., the tombs at Kalimari in the Phaestos region, and Kefalas Teke at Gypsades in the Knossos region—in their long evolution have gradually been discovered. The two royal tombs found at Knossos—although stripped of almost all their contents—had some noteworthy peculiarities. The tomb of Isopata contained a rectangular chamber covered by a saddle-backed roof, and niches on either side of the entrance; while the Southern Royal Tomb was a two-storeyed building with a porticoed court, a vestibule, a crypt sanctuary, and a sepulchral chamber cut deeply into the rock—in short, it was similar to the legendary tomb of Minos in Sicily which was connected with a shrine of Aphrodite. Most of the communal tombs were tombs with chambers, pits, or cists, very similar to those in the Mycenaean region of mainland Greece. *Larnakes*, shaped like chests or bathtubs, were usually placed inside these tombs.

Mural painting and pottery

It was natural that the Minoan delight in the picturesque should find such fine expression in the mural decorations that contributed so much to the splendour and charm of the palaces. Not only the walls but often the ceilings and floors were decorated with paintings, even in villas and country houses and simple town dwellings. Unfortunately only fragments of these paintings have survived. Notwithstanding their occasional conventionality, the forceful lines and luminous colours of these frescoes express the Minoans' *joie de vivre* and feeling for nature. The subjects were drawn mainly from marine and land plants, religious ceremonies, and the gay life of the court and the people. The worship of nature pervaded everything. The recurrent theme of the Minoan bull games may also have had religious significance. The treatment is full of charm and lyrical feeling. It was not until this final phase that a preference for symmetry and regularity prevailed. But the decorative motifs based on the spiral and the rosette never became static.

The study of New Palace pottery has greatly contributed to our general knowledge of the period. In its development are reflected not only the progress of Minoan civilization but the influences that acted on it and the differences between various regions. The Old Palace polychrome decoration gradually developed into a monochrome type using white on a violet or maroon ground and with an increasing predilection for subjects drawn from the plant world and marine fauna. This change naturally led to a return to the style of dark decorations on a light ground which enhanced the effect of the designs drawn from nature and facilitated their adaptation to the shape of the vase. Polychrome decoration was confined to highlights in white and bands of orange. Decorative motifs of spirals, rosettes, garlands, and sacred symbols were used, either on separate bands or painted over the whole surface. A large number of new forms were influenced by prototypes in metal. Vessels for religious purposes (e. g., rhytons) or for the export of liquids (e. g., the curious "stirrup" vases) were widely used. Under the influence of the new Mycenaean spirit from the north, decoration in the so-called palace style became more formal and conventional, though the subjects remained the same. A vast quantity of everyday vessels and objects in common use, especially cooking utensils (griddles, pots, sieves, funnels, etc.), have been brought to light by the excavations.

Seal- and gem-engraving
The more grandiose arts such as monumental sculpture were alien to the whole spirit of the Minoans. They loved graceful things and excelled in small-scale carving and seal-engraving for which they used a variety of materials such as clay, stone, metal, ivory, and faience. Production in these fields generally consisted of religious objects such as figurines of gods, votive statuettes of worshippers and sacrificial animals, models of sanctuaries and religious ceremonies, vases with carvings in relief, etc. These are astonishingly varied, the material is skilfully handled, and there is no lack of expression and movement. Outstanding skill is shown in some of the three-dimensional groups in which the figures are presented in action; the most interesting of these are the compositions in ivory or metal of scenes from the *Taurokathapsia*. Especially graceful are the figures of women in sumptuous dresses and sophisticated hairstyles; these are most delightful when they are executed in iridescent faience. In stone work, beautiful vases were produced, most of them masterpieces in exquisite taste. The most perfect examples were found in the treasuries of sanctuaries—vessels in the shape of sacred animals or animal heads, mostly bulls and lions, chalices cut from semi-precious stones, rhytons with fine carvings in which the veining of the stone is skilfully used, vases modelled in metal-work, and vases with reliefs showing sanctuaries, rituals, athletic contests, sacred emblems, etc. The materials most commonly used were alabaster, basalt, obsidian, porphyry, rock crystal, malachite, and various veined marbles. Steatite vases with reliefs were often covered with gold-leaf to give the effect of precious metal. Other objects, such as lamps, were shaped like the calices of flowers, sheaves of papyrus, or shells. Shaped vases and altar

166

ornaments were sometimes in faience. The most important series of stone and faience objects were found in the palaces of Knossos and Zakro.

The Minoan talent for miniature work found a perfect medium in seal-engraving, as we know from the large number of seals that have survived and from the many imprints that have been preserved on clay. On minute round or elliptical surfaces they contrived to depict a world of action and movement, taking their subjects from nature or religion. Notwithstanding the distortions that sometimes resulted from the use of round frames, they created microscopic works of art. All sorts of stone were used, including semi-precious and even precious ones.

Metal-working
Outstanding progress was made in all branches of metal work. Thanks to improved techniques, vases could be skilfully shaped and decorated with inlays, engravings, or repoussé work. Relatively few vases in precious metals have been found on the island, but this is because the palaces had frequently been pillaged and no royal tomb has so far been discovered intact. On the other hand, the vases found in Mycenaean Greece came from Crete and were of Cretan workmanship. Moreover, the bronze vessels excavated in Crete have their exact equivalents in early Mycenaean vessels, such as tripods, cauldrons, wash-basins, amphorae, etc. Although the Minoans were an exceptionally peace-loving people, considerable progress was made in the manufacture of weapons. By laminating and hammering they managed to produce the longest swords known in prehistoric times. The blades were reinforced with fine ribs and the hilt was often made of precious material, set off by finely wrought decoration on gold laminations. The technique of damascening produced splendid daggers on which inlays of fine threads of precious metal or black enamel depicted scenes full of movement. A great many such daggers were found in the royal tombs at Mycenae and in the Pylos region; it is certain that this technique was first

practised in Crete, although only a single dagger with an inlay—depicting a hunting scene—has been found there. Bronze helmets with cheek pieces and leather helmets decorated with bands of boar's tusks have also been found in Crete. Such helmets were often pictured in works of art and there seems to be no reason for thinking that they originated in the north. Heavy figure-of-eight shields made of layers of ox-hide and reinforced by a metal framework, often appear in pictures, but no actual remains of these shields have been identified with certainty.

The talent for miniature work also produced a wealth of masterpieces in gold and silver work. The techniques of gold and silver working—laminating, the preparation of alloys, welding, inlay, filigree and granulation—attained perfection. All manner of jewellery was manufactured—gold rings with minute religious scenes on the bezels, necklaces with pendants in the shape of flowers, sea creatures, fruit, bull's heads, lion cubs, gazelles, etc., hairpins tipped with flowers, exquisitely wrought ornaments representing gods or sacred animals (the best known of these is the bee pendant from Mallia), diadems with repoussé decoration, ear-rings in the shape of ox-heads, amulets with minute magical images, and many more. The jewellery was generally extremely graceful and most delicately worked. When these jewels—especially the necklaces—were worn with ornaments of different material and colour, for instance with semi-precious stones, their beauty must have been further enhanced, and we can well imagine how effective they must have been on the graceful Minoan women. We also know something of this from the paintings that have survived. Unfortunately, nearly all objects made of perishable material have been destroyed by the damp Cretan climate. Our only information on a great many crafts —weaving, embroidery, tapestry work, leather work, glass manufacture, cabinet making, and to a great extent, inlaying— comes from the pictures of them that have survived. To judge from some of the pictures, all these crafts must have been highly developed and added greatly to the brilliance of Minoan civilization.

1

111

112 →

Social and political life

Archaeologists have tried to form some idea of the kind of life the Minoans led during the latest palace period, for which more evidence is available than for any of the earlier ones. Scholars pinned great hopes on the decipherment of the texts written in the Linear A and Linear B scripts, although they knew beforehand that the contents were limited to a special subject. When the texts had been successfully deciphered it became clear that the numerous tablets in Linear B threw some light on the final phase of life in the palace at Knossos—the Achaean phase, as it turned out—but gave no help whatever with the preceding periods. It was thought that more might be learnt about these if the few Linear A texts, which had been transcribed, could only be understood. As it is, scholars have reconciled themselves to the fact that they must rely on the evidence of the excavations alone, that is, on the material remains of the Minoan civilization. Here we can only briefly summarize their findings about the social and political life of the New Palace period.

Although it would be misleading to describe it as a matriarchy, there is a great deal of evidence—even from later Hellenic times—that the succession passed through the female line. The dominant role played by women in society is shown by the fact that they took an active part in all aspects of New Palace life. This may have been due to the absence of the men on long sea journeys. The *genos* seems no longer to have occupied the foremost place in the organization of society. Social classes—peasants, craftsmen, priests, magistrates—had come into being, and the balance between them seems to have been maintained by a hierarchy headed by the king. There are reasons to believe that the organization of society and politics was profoundly influenced by religion, and it is possible that a wholly theocratic form of government had evolved in which the kings ruled as representatives of the deity, their palaces being the dwelling of the gods and the taxes they levied an offering of first-fruits. The feudal system—land tenure in return for services to the king—revealed by the tablets undoubtedly dated back to the peak period. The authority of the king was probably limited by councils of high officials, on which other social classes may have been represented. The maintenance of order depended on peaceful relations between the kings of the island, who ruled by divine authority and were therefore bound to govern in accordance with the divine will and to avoid abuse of power. Supreme justice must also have been in the hands of the king, and the tradition which recounts that King Minos ruled and dispensed justice according to divinely ordained laws is a reflection of the theocratic system that prevailed. The Throne Room at Knossos with its ceremonial features seems to have been a sort of sacred court, and the underground rooms with benches discovered near the palace of Mallia have been regarded as a sort of senate hall where the king-priest sat in council. There are references in Homer to such councils in the kingdom of Nestor at Pylos. There are many indications that there was a class of slaves, but they do not seem to have been very numerous or very active and they did not create any social problems. The standard of living—even of the peasants—seems to have been high. None of the homes found so far have suggested very poor living conditions. No doubt the long period of "peaceful co-existence" benefited the country. It seems quite possible that this society included a group of foreigners who had settled on the island for trade or other purposes and who took an active part in the life of the country. The priests were undoubtedly very powerful, to judge from the large buildings they erected in the immediate vicinity of the palaces, but their power never seems to have become a threat to the king—as it did in Egypt—for the king himself was always the high priest and was often portrayed wearing priestly insignia. Even the queen and princes took part in the religious rites and held high priestly offices.

The existence of archives keeping orderly accounts shows that the administration was organized on bureaucratic lines. The innumerable store-rooms and sanctuary treasuries indicate that the king, as high priest, administered the public funds, and probably extensive public and maintenance works were financed out of the tribute collected each year in the name of the deity. It is difficult to tell how the administrative and military hierarchy was organized, how order was maintained, and what kind of army and navy the state possessed. We have very little information on the shape of the ships, the weapons, the use of chariots, the introduction of horses, the recruitment of negroes, and perhaps mercenaries, in the army, etc.

Economic life

Agriculture, stock-breeding, industry, and trade, all contributed to the economic prosperity of the country and raised the standard of living. The carbonized remains that have been found of the produce of the soil and the implements used in its cultivation and preservation show that a wide range of crops was produced. These included notably olives, vines, cereals, vegetables, and fruits. All kinds of implements have been found, very similar to those used today but made of bronze, except for the ploughs which seem to have been made of wood. Various sorts of wine- and oil-presses and assortments or mortars and pestles have been found, mostly in Minoan country houses. The Minoans had several varieties of vine as is shown by the different kinds of grape seeds. Apples, pears, and figs were the favourite fruits. Aromatic seeds and herbs were gathered carefully, and in Greece many of them bear pre-Hellenic names to this day.

That bee-keeping was practised we know from certain pictures, from the fact that the bee was used as a decorative motif, and from special containers in the shape of stylized bee-hives. The tablets mention that jars of honey were offered to the goddess Eileithyia. There were more species of domestic animals than before, and there is much evidence that large-scale breeding of cattle, sheep, goats, pigs, etc. was carried on. The bones found during excavations show that there was a great variety of animals in Crete, used either for breeding or hunting. We do not know to what degree fishing was organized, but there are many pictures of fish being caught, and hooks of all sizes have been found. Livestock products provided not only food but were used for the manufacture of clothes; hemp and flax were also cultivated for the production of textiles.

The large number of manufactured objects brought to light by excavations have taught us a great deal about all branches of industry.

We know exactly what raw materials and instruments were used, we know the installations of the various workshops and the techniques practised. We know now that copper came from Cyprus, gold from Nubia, tin from Anatolia, ivory from the Syrian countries, obsidian from Melos, basalt from Laconia, papyrus and palm-trees from Egypt, cedar from Lebanon, cornelian from Cornwall in England, etc. The island itself had rich ore deposits and plenty of timber, cypress being the wood most commonly used.

Trade with the civilized countries of the Near East and Egypt had been methodically extended, and we know that manufactured articles from Crete and the excellent wines and oil were in great demand. In exchange Crete received raw materials and precious metals. It seems that most of the trade was in the hands of the kings who may even have enjoyed a monopoly of it. Shipping had made great progress, and we know from the numerous pictures of ships that a large fleet had been assembled. The founding of the chief ports and trading posts dates from this peak period which also marked the real beginning of colonization and thalassocracy. Each day fresh discoveries confirm the tremendous colonial expansion that occurred during this period. There were Cretan settlements in the islands, in Melos, Thera, Kea, the northern Sporades, and Rhodes, and also in Phoenicia at Ungarit and at Minet el Beyda; systematic excavations have shown that countless Minoan objects were brought to these places. This colonial expansion is connected with the origin of the Mycenaean civilization, and the subject will be treated more fully in a later volume of *Archaeologia Mundi*. Here we can only say that the sudden birth of a civilization such as the Mycenaean cannot be satisfactorily explained in terms of an invasion of Crete by the middle-Helladic Achaeans whose civilization until then had been rudimentary. Research will show whether the colonial expansion of the Minoans had carried them to some, of the nerve-centres of the western Mediterranean.

Private life
Archaeological evidence suggests that private life in this period had attained a high level of refinement and comfort. The houses were adapted to all practical needs of life, and an attractive environment was created round them. The Minoans were very close to nature, and their architecture was designed to let them enjoy it as freely as possible while adapting their houses to the semi-tropical climate of Crete. Gardens were laid out round houses and especially palaces, and sometimes even inside them; flowers in a host of decorated vases expressed the Minoan awareness of the presence of nature. Special walks, porticos, retreats, terraces, even bathrooms with hot water were designed for convenience and relaxation. Children had their own apartments, often with small baths. Clothes—light loincloths for men, sumptuous dresses for women leaving the breast bare and emphasizing the slimness of the waist—allowed the body suppleness and freedom of movement. Hats with narrow or broad brims might be worn, or the head left bare and the hair arranged in artistic styles. Beauty aids were used much as they are today—make-up, eye-shadow, depilatories, hair curlers, powder, scent, etc.—and the muscles were strengthened and toned by physical exercises.

Even the nobility took to artistic work, and the ladies of the court busied themselves with weaving and embroidery. Leisure hours would be spent in games of backgammon or other amusements, while music, singing, and dancing added to the pleasures of life. The main musical instruments were the many-stringed lyre and the flute. There were frequent public ceremonies and festivals, mostly religious, accompanied by processions, banquets, and acrobatic displays performed in theatres built for the purpose or in wooden arenas. To these entertainments must be added the dangerous *taurokathar-psia* or bull games.

Religion

Archaeological findings concerning the religious life of the New Palace period are especially important because of the vital part played by religion in the Minoan world. The interpretation of the evidence has, however, been the subject of a great deal of controversy. This is hardly surprising, since there are so many unknown factors. But there is plenty of material, and from the study of comparative religion, the investigation of surviving traditions and of religious ideas in Crete during the pre-Hellenic period, and finally from the examination of pre-Hellenic elements in the Creto-Mycenaean texts a clearer general picture is beginning to emerge. The Minoan deities seem to have been confined to a few figures personifying the creative and ruling forces in nature. Such facts as we know—the type of places chosen for sanctuaries, the sacred symbols, the attendant animals, the form of the ceremonies, the surviving rites—suggest that there probably were two chief creative figures, the powerful male god and the fertile mother, and two others—the son and daughter—who personified the cycle of death and rebirth in nature. They were worshipped in three spheres, celestial, terrestrial and subterranean. We do not know whether these figures had as yet become separate gods or whether they were still worshipped as different manifestations of the same basic deities in the three different spheres. Goddesses, as the productive deities, were considered the most important. In art they are portrayed in their various aspects, as the Queen of Wild Beasts, Kourotrophos (Nursing Mother of Youths), Mother and Daughter, the Goddess of the Serpents, and the Goddess of the Doves. The figure of a child or youth, sometimes shown with the Mother Goddess, has been identified —by analogy with similar figures found in the East—as the son and lover of the goddess. This interpretation has also been confirmed by later tradition, and echoes of it are found in the cycle of the Hellenic mysteries; further evidence for it has lately been found in the Creto-Mycenaean tablets. We might expect that Cretan art would also portray a powerful father-god, the fertilizer of the great goddess; his absence, combined with the important part played by the worship of the bull, suggests that the bull symbolized the male creative force and that the god was worshipped in this form. This is supported by the later Creto-Hellenic tradition in which bull-gods are coupled with figures like Europa and Pasiphae who must originally have been goddesses. In the celestial sphere the bull-god is symbolized by the disc of the sun and the golden horn of the crescent moon. His presence was also felt in the other spheres, especially that of the netherworld. He is the "earth-shaker" responsible for the geological upheavals so frequent in Minoan Crete. Undoubtedly he was also the sovereign master of the waters and the sea; in the tablets he is called Potidas (later Poseidon), the Lord of the Earth. Two young couples (the Diaskouroi and Dioskouroi) appeared at the side of the deity. Both were to survive into later periods.

It seems that the Minoan gods generally assumed human or animal forms, but they could also appear in aniconic form—that is, neither human nor animal—and were probably believed to inhabit such objects as pillars, columns, or stalactites which were thereby transformed into bethels or dwellings of the gods. The cycle of the seasons was regarded as a sacred drama which later seems to have formed the basis of the mysteries. We find many representations of the uprooting of the sacred tree, accompanied by tears and lamentations, and of the resurrection of the young god amidst the ecstatic dances of spring. There is also some evidence for a tradition of the abduction and return of the young Maiden—yet another symbol of the cycle of vegetation. These ideas lived on in Greek religion, especially in the mystery cults.

It would be difficult to give these deities their true names from among those that have survived in Cretan mythology and religion or are mentioned in the tablets. Some of them seem to be genuinely pre-Hellenic—e.g., Eileithyia, Dictynna, Eleuthia, Britomartis, Akakallis, while others—such as Europa and Pasiphae, "the dark" and the "bright"—seem to be Greek translations. The names Anassai and Eleuthia occur in the tablets.

The sites for Minoan places of worship were determined by the nature of the gods they were built to honour: thus celestial deities were worshipped on the tops of mountains or hills, terrestrial ones had their shrines in palaces, houses in the country, or on the sea shore, while the subterranean gods were worshipped in the depth of caves. Occasionally animals attended on the gods or became their substitutes: birds were associated with the celestial deities, land animals, wild beasts, and sea creatures with the terrestrial gods, and snakes and scarabs with the underground ones. The symbols, too, corresponded to these three spheres, the chief ones being the double-headed axe and the sacred horns, the disc or wheel of the sun, and the crescent moon. There were rites involving sacrifices, processions, performances of the sacred drama of germination, the transport of altars by boat from one seaside sanctuary to another, etc. Festivals included athletic and acrobatic displays and bull games. Dancing and music had an important place in worship, especially dancing with the state of ecstasy, conducive to contact with the deity, it produced. The highest offices of the priesthood were filled by members of the royal family, while the priestesses formed its principal order. There was also a category of priests who wore women's clothes.

We do not know what part was played by the demons who are portrayed in so many religious pictures. They probably acted as mediators between man and the gods. All sorts of outlandish composite monsters of this type were engraved on seals, but we do not know to what extent these images represented an actual belief. Such supernatural creatures as the griffin, the sphinx, and an odd quadruped with a long neck had a different signifiance and belonged to an imagery that probably stemmed from Egypt and the East.

184

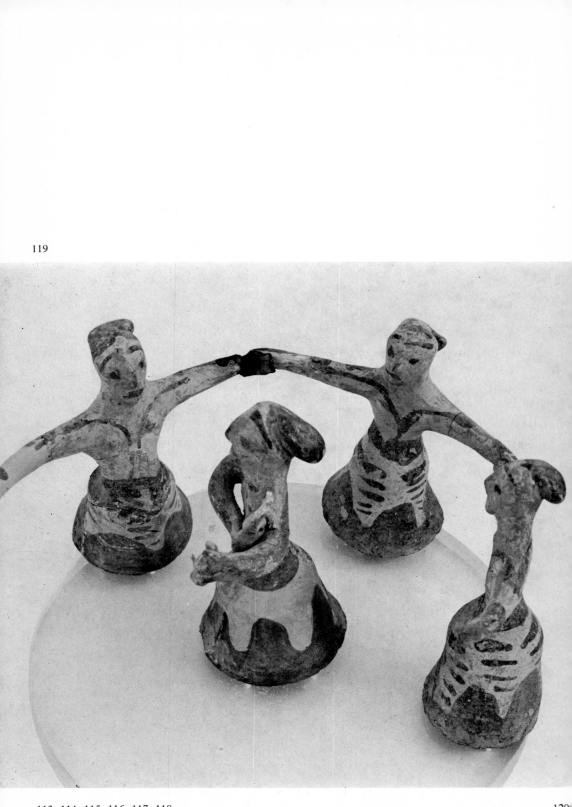

123

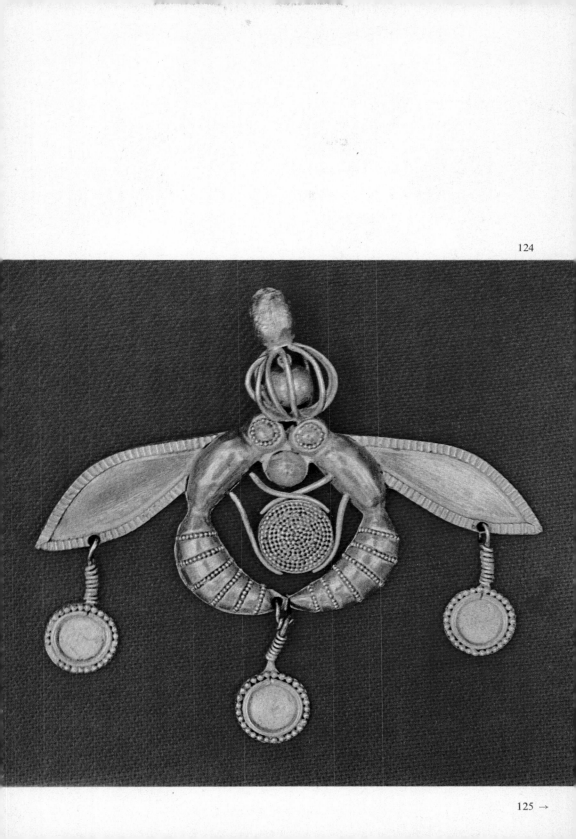

125 →

The Minoans also retained a strong belief in magic, by which they sought to compel gods or demons to intervene favourably or malevolently in human affairs; the use of talismans was also widespread.

Burial rites and the worship of the dead

Minoan burial customs during the New Palace period tell us a great deal about the beliefs of the time concerning an after-life. The tombs and their contents show that there had been a general rise in the level of civilization. Funerary rites were performed to ensure the unhindered passage of the dead into the world beyond. Provisions were laid down for the journey. To these were added libations and commemorative offerings, and as these rites were founded on a belief in the supernatural powers of the dead they gradually developed into a form of worship. In a way, all the dead were raised to the status of saints, while the dead kings—whom the gods received as their own— were deified. This we know from pictures and images and from the form of worship of the dead which differed little from that used in honour of the gods. The paintings on the famous sarcophagus of Hagia Triada have provided a great deal of information on this subject. They show that sacrifices were performed in honour of the dead, the sprinkling of libations to recall him to life and summon him forth, and the propitatory offerings that followed. The transformation of the burial chamber and of the tomb into a sanctuary was characteristic of this period. In the use of blue for colouring the roof of the tomb and the bier, there is perhaps a symbolic allusion to the celestial world of the Elysian Fields.

The final destruction

All the evidence points unequivocally to the fact that the total and universal destruction of the new palaces by geological upheavals occurred towards 1450 B.C. This date has been established on the basis of comparisons with evidence from Egypt and the Near East. Moreover, conclusive evidence has recently been found to confirm the view held by Professor S. Marinatos that the destruction was caused by the eruption of the volcano of Santorini and the resulting earth-tremors. Large pieces of volcanic lava have been found in the palace at Zakro and piles of pumice stone on other parts of the coast. After this catastrophe only Knossos seems to have survived, and life there continued until about 1380 B.C. under Achaean rule, as the decipherment of the tablets has shown. But it is impossible to believe that the whole of the rest of Crete was deserted. Groups of people must have gone on living—in small settlements, probably, that have not yet been located. This question became hotly controversial when the philologist Leonard Palmer put forward the theory that the palace at Knossos survived as a brilliant Achaean-Mycenaean political and administrative centre beyond 1200 B.C. and claimed that the archives compiled in Linear B dated from that period. If this were true, it would have to be assumed that Evans, the excavator of Knossos, misused or falsified the archaeological evidence to lend support to his preconceived ideas. Palmer subsequently published extracts from the original diary and notes of the excavation, especially those relating to the discovery of the tablets. The archaeologist John Boardman strongly opposed Palmer's theory, and the controversy, often acrimonious, continues to this day with supporters on both sides. In my own opinion, the historical and archaeological facts do not support Palmer's theory, but further excavations must be carried out at Knossos if we want to have a decisive confirmation of Evans' views. In that case we may find that the new Achaean dynasty had settled in palaces outside the destroyed Minoan palaces and that the latter—as Evans maintained—had been only partially and sporadically reoccupied.

Post-Palace Crete

Post-Palace settlements

Even after the destruction of the great palace centres, Minoan life continued unchanged along the same lines as before, and a variety of works of art were still produced in every field. However, as the Achaean settlements increased, Minoan culture took on a markedly Mycenaean character. It would be wrong to consider this period as one of general decline, for the standard of civilization and achievement remained high, and large mixed Minoan-Mycenaean towns grew up, as is shown by the remains found at Phaestos, Tylissos, Hagia Triada, Khondros Viannos, and Gournia. Buildings of a new type and style have been discovered there: colonnaded agoras with two storeys and shops, Mycenaean megarons and porticos, separate chapels that seemed to be forerunners of the temple (at Hagia Triada), vast buildings with paved squares, altars and porticos, and cisterns (at Tylissos), and houses built to an original plan (at Khondros and Gournia). Small chapels were sometimes erected on the site of the old sanctuaries, the ruined palaces and large private houses, and other, similar chapels were built out of doors. The best known of these shrines are those of the Double-headed Axe, of the Fetish Symbols, and of the Covered Spring at Knossos, that in the Villa of Gortyna, and a number of others at Gournia, Hagia Triada, and Koumasa. Unfortunately most of these settlements have not yet been explored, but the large number of necropoles with carved and domed tombs suggest that Crete was still fairly densely populated during this period. The necropoles have a distinctly Mycenaean character.

Decline in the arts
Although artistic production continued without any basic change, a new spirit nevertheless began to pervade the regions under Mycenaean influence; mass production led to simplification and standardization. This was particularly noticeable in pottery which adopted the so-called common style *("koine")* throughout the whole Mycenaean world, Techniques had been greatly improved (faster wheels, flawless firing, careful fining down and smoothing of the clay, application of slip and lustrous paint). But the new symmetrical designs and abstract decoration rendered the old naturalistic subjects unrecognizable. Even representative subjects such as hunts, chariots, or water fowl, were treated in such a stylized way that many of

their features became mere conventional forms. In its final phase, pottery was greatly simplified, and only the so-called close style, influenced by the eastern Mediterranean islands, revived the old motifs, though it smothered them in an exuberance of decoration. For vases only the most useful shapes were retained, such as vessels for banquets, tall-stemmed cups and mixing bowls, and receptacles for commercial use such as amphorae and flasks.

Terracotta sculpture underwent the greatest stylization. Figurines deteriorated into grotesques, but there were also some interesting new types of idols, fairly large, with a cylindrical body, and arms raised at right angles, and with symbols or sacred animals on the head and in the hands. The most important series of such figurines came from Knossos, Ghazi, Prinia and Karphi.

No significant progress was achieved in the other branches of art, which followed the old Minoan tradition or wholly adapted themselves to the new Mycenaean spirit without, however, accomplishing anything comparable to what was achieved in the main centres of Mycenaean civilization. On the whole, the work was provincial.

It is a strange fact that during this period the civilization spread to the whole of the island and had many centres in western Crete which, oddly enough, had remained practically uninhabited during the golden age of Minoan culture. Admittedly, the region had not been as totally deserted as was thought originally, and numerous remains are now being discovered some of which date back to the early Minoan periods.

Mycenaean Crete
If the numerous Linear B tablets could definitively be assigned to the Post-Palace period, they would tell us a great deal about life in this final phase. From them emerges the picture of a feudal society ruled by a centralized

government. This question will be discussed more fully in the volume of *Archaeologia Mundi* devoted to the Mycenaean world. Many features of the social organization must have survived the destruction of the palace at Knossos and may have continued, in a modified form, in the new Mycenaean State which finally became involved in the Trojan War in the reign of Idomeneus. However, this is purely hypothetical and has not been proved, although it seems very probable. In fact, we know very little about life during this period. The only conclusion we can draw from the available data—and this seems logical—is that the Minoan and Mycenaean elements in Crete became fused and that the Mycenaean character predominated, producing a common, Mycenaean way of life. The Achaean governors must have been fairly autonomous and adapted their manner of living to that of the rest of the Mycenaean world.

Cretan trade no longer played an important part, for the sea routes and markets were in the hands of the new Mycenaean powers of mainland Greece and the dependent Aegean islands. Nevertheless, Crete was rich, and the intensive cultivation of the soil produced enough to feed the growing population. But its resistance was weakened and it could offer no opposition to the sudden Dorian invasion. The ancient faith had gone out of its religion which was no more than a jumble of old beliefs and Minoan forms of worship and the new anthropocentric beliefs of the Homeric age.

The migration of the Peoples of the Sea and the Dorian invasion
The Dorian invasion was undoubtedly the principal cause of the migration of so-called the Peoples of the Sea. Their last wave reached Egypt and established settlements on the south-east coast of Asia Minor, in southern Phoenicia, and in Cyprus. The Dorian invasion also caused an upheaval in Crete. The island was too weak to offer any resistance to the invaders. The latter destroyed the remaining Mycenaean centres and drove the inhabitants into the montainous regions in the centre and east. The last places of refuge of the native population have been discovered on naturally forti-

fied heights, e. g., at Karphi and in the Lassithi mountains, and at Vrocastro and Kavousi in the mountain ranges of eastern Crete. They had become a sub-Minoan society of mountain brigands, raiding the Dorian settlements in the plain. For a time the Creto-Mycenaean tradition was kept alive, but it was finally engulfed by the nascent Proto-geometric culture. The sub-Minoan phase survived somewhat longer among the so-called Eteocretans— the genuine Cretans—in the region of Sitia where the Minoan language was spoken until well into the age of classical Greece, although it was written in Greek characters. In the plains, the Dorians at first settled in small groups of purely military units; they introduced their own civilization which was characterized by the use of a new metal, iron, by the cremation of the dead, the wearing of a new type of garment made of a single piece of cloth which was draped round the body and fastened with a buckle, and, in pottery, by the use of abstract geometric designs. Their military conquest of the island progressed fairly slowly, and during this period they were compelled to settle in fortified acropoles from which they controlled the plain and to organize themselves into a military state in which the citizens had to undergo severe military training. After the complete subjection of the island, a measure of agreement was reached with the old Minoan and Achaean population within the framework of the new Dorian order, and the surviving pre-Hellenic and proto-Hellenic influence began to make itself felt. Crete became receptive to influences from the East, and this opened the way to the miracle of the birth of Greek civilization. Once again the island demonstrated its amazing vitality and became one of the chief centres of the maturing new civilization. Tradition has linked the island with the name of Daedalus, the legendary craftsman, a personification of the adventurous Minoan genius.

History and legend
Echoes of the vanished Golden Age of the Minoans have come down to us through the dark Geometric "middle ages" in which even the skill of writing was forgotten. Historical realities can be discerned on closer exami-

nation of the legends in which they are shrouded. The legends of Minos, Sarpedon, and Rhadamanthus have been linked with the palaces of Knossos, Mallia, and Phaestos; the Labyrinth represents the intricate layout of the palace of Knossos, the place where the double-headed axes were kept; the bitter fight with the Minotaur may have been an echo of the Minoan bull games; the story of the thalassocracy of Minos and the Cretan colonial settlements have sometimes been confirmed in detail as historical facts. We know, too, that the technical skills ascribed to the Telchines and Daedalus had foundations in reality. Minoan religious beliefs are reflected in Greek mythology, and the connexion between Minoan Crete and the oldest Greek sanctuaries has been conclusively proved. The famous story of the expeditions of Minos to Megaris and Sicily had a historical basis. The tradition of the conflict between Knossos and the Mycenaean kingdom of Athens—echoed in the myth of Atlantis—no longer seems purely fictitious, while the Achaean settlements in Crete, mentioned in other fables, are known to be historical facts. We know, too, that the myths of the land of the Phaeaces and of the Golden Age were based on distant memories of the prodigious civilization of Crete.

CONCLUSION

The excavations undertaken in Crete so far have helped us to solve a good many of the problems with which we were faced at the outset. In the meantime, new problems have arisen and have been solved in turn or at least are approaching their solution. Minoan archaeology has helped us to obtain a fairly clear and complete picture of a civilization that has only recently been discovered. It has shown the important contribution made by the Minoans to the birth of the Greek civilization that succeeded them, and through the Greeks to the shaping of our contemporary world. Admittedly, there are still many problems to be solved. There is no doubt that further excavations will raise fresh questions and that these, in turn, will be answered. With each step we are learning more about the history of Man, and what has been achieved up to the present augurs well for the future progress of the science of archaeology.

CHRONOLOGICAL TABLE OF MINOAN CIVILIZATION

Nicolas Platon's chronology	Absolute chronology	Comparison with Sir Arthur Evans' chronology	Comparison with Egyptian chronology	Comparison with Mesopotamian chronology
Neolithic Age	B.C.	*Neolithic Age*	*Predynastic* (before 3100 B.C.)	Periods of Hassuna, Samarra, Halaf (5th mill. B. C.)
Early Neolithic I	6000–4000 ?	Early Neolithic		Ubaid Period (ca. 3500 B.C.)
EarlyNeolithic II		Middle Neolithic		
Middle Neolithic	4000–3000 ?	Late Neolithic	*Protodynastic* 1st–3rd Dynasty (3100–2612 B.C.)	Jemdet Nasr Period (ca. 3000 B.C.)
Late Neolithic	3000–2600 ?			
Pre-Palace Period		*Early Minoan*	*Early Kingdom*	First Dynasty of Ur (ca. 2500 B.C.)
Phase I	2600–2400	Early Minoan I	4th–6th Dynasty (2612–2280 B.C.)	Period of Akkad (2400–2200 B.C.)
Phase II	2400–2200	Early Minoan II		Invasion of the Guti (ca. 2200 B.C.)
		Early Minoan III	*1st Intermediate Period*	Neo-Sumerian Period (ca. 2100 B.C.)
Phase III	2200–2000	*Middle Minoan*	7th–10th Dynasty (ca. 2280–2040 B.C.)	
		Middle Minoan I a		

PROTOMINOAN AGE

MINOAN AGE

	B.C.		Egypt	Mesopotamia
Old Palace Period			*Middle Kingdom*	Third Dynasty of Ur
Phase I	2000–1900	Middle Minoan 1 b	11th–13th Dynasty (2133–1625 B.C.)	
Phase II	1900–1800	Middle Minoan II a		First Dynasty of Babylon (1894–1585 B.C.)
Phase III	1800–1700	Middle Minoan II b		Hammurabi (1792–1750 B.C.)
New Palace Period			*2nd Intermediate Period* (Hyksos)	
Phase I	1700–1600	Middle Minoan III a, b	14th–17th Dynasty (1720–1527 B.C.)	
Phase II	1600–1450	*Late Minoan* Late Minoan I a, b	*New Kingdom* 18th Dynasty (1570–1320 B.C.)	
Phase III	1450–1400	Late Minoan II		
Post-Palace Period				Kassite Dynasty (1595–1155)
Phase I	1400–1320	Late Minoan III a		
Phase II	1320–1260	Late Minoan III b	19th Dynasty (1320–1200 B.C.)	
Phase III	1260–1150	Late Minoan III b	20th Dynasty (1200–1085 B.C.)	Tiglath-Pileser I King of Assyria and Babylonia (1116–1078 B.C.)
Subminoan Age	1150–1000	*Subminoan*		

207

BIBLIOGRAPHY

Only the principal works and monographs are listed here. They contain detailed bibliographies that will enable the reader to pursue the subject further.

I. General

BANTI (L.), PUGLIESE CARRATELLI (G.), LEVI (D.), *Arte Minoica e Micenea*, Enciclopedia dell'Arte Antica Classica e Orientale, Vol. V, 42 ss.

BOSSERT (H.), *Alt-Kreta*, [3] Berlin 1937, The Art of Ancient Crete, 1937.

CHARBONNEAUX (J.), *L'Art égéen*, Paris 1923.

CHILDE (V.G.), *The Dawn of European Civilization*, [2] London 1950.

DEMARGNE (P.), *La Crète dédalique*, Paris 1947.

DEMARGNE (P.), *Naissance de l'art grec*, Paris 1964.

DUSSAUD (R.), *Les civilisations préhelléniques dans le bassin de la mer Egée*, [2] Paris 1914.

EVANS (Sir Arthur), *The Palace of Minos*, Vol. I–IV, London, 1921–1935.

FIMMEN (D.), *Die kretisch-mykenische Kultur*, [2] Leipzig-Berlin 1924.

FORSDYKE (J.), *Minoan Art*, Proceedings of the British Academy 15, London 1929.

GLOTZ (G.), *La Civilisation égéenne*, [2] Paris 1952.

GRAHAM (J.W.), *The Palaces of Crete*, Princeton 1962.

HALL (H.R.), *The Civilization of Greece in the Bronze Age*, London 1928.

HUTCHINSON (R.), *Prehistoric Crete*, Penguin Books, London 1962.

KARO (G.), *Kreta*, in Pauly-Wissowa Realencyclopädie.

KARO (G.), *Greifen am Thron, Erinnerungen an Knossos*, Baden-Baden 1959.

MARINATOS (Sp.), HIRMER (M.), *Kreta und das mykenische Hellas*, München 1959.

MATZ (Fr.), *Die Ägäis*, in *Handbuch der Archäologie II*, 1950, 179 ff.

MATZ (Fr.), *Kreta, Mykene, Troja*, Stuttgart 1958.

MATZ (Fr.), *Kreta und frühes Griechenland*, Baden-Baden 1962.

MATZ (Fr.), *Minoan Civilization*, in Cambridge Ancient History, 1962.

MONTELIUS (O.), *La Grèce préclassique I–II*, Stockholm 1924–1928.

PENDLEBURY (J.D.S.), *The Archaeology of Crete*, London 1939.

PLATON (N.), *Cretese-Miceneo* in Enciclopedia Universale dell'Arte IV; 70 ss.

PRASCHNIKER (C.), *Kretische Kunst*, 1921.

SCHACHERMEYR (Fr.), *Die prähistorischen Kulturen Griechenlands*, in Pauly-Wissowa Realenc. 22, 1954.

SCHACHERMEYR (Fr.), *Die ältesten Kulturen Griechenlands*, Stuttgart 1955.

SCHACHERMEYR (Fr.), *Die minoische Kultur des alten Kreta*, Stuttgart 1964.

SNIJDER (G.), *Kretische Kunst*, Berlin 1936.

SCHWEITZER (B.), *Altkretische Kunst*, in Antike II, 1926, 191 ss.
THOMPSON (G.), *The Prehistoric Aegean*, [2] London 1954.
ZERVOS (Chr.), *L'art de la Crète néolithique et minoenne*, Paris 1956.

II. Sites

Knossos EVANS (Sir Arthur), *The Palace of Minos*, Vol. I–IV, London 1921–1935.
    Prehistoric Tombs of Knossos, in Archaeologia LIX, London 1906.
    The Tomb of the Double Axes, in Archaeologia LXV, London 1914.
    EVANS (J.), *Excavations in the Neolithic Mound of Knossos*, in Bulletin of the Institute of Archaeology 4, 1964.
    Excavations in the Neolithic Settlement of Knossos in British School Annual, 59, 1964, 152 ss.
    FURNESS (Mrs Ozanne), *The Neolithic Pottery of Knossos*, in British School Annual 48, 1953, 94 ss.
Phaestos PERNIER (L.), *Il Palazzo Minoico di Festos*, *I*, Roma 1935, *II* (with BANTI (L.), 1951.
    LEVI (D.), *Plusieurs articles sur les nouvelles fouilles depuis 1951* in Annuario della Scuola Italiana di Atene and in Bollettino d'Arte and Parola del Passato.
Mallia *Rapports préliminaires* in the Series on Cretan Studies since 1928 (especially CHAPOUTHIER (F.), DEMARGNE (P.), GALLET DE SANTERRE (H.), DESHAYES (J.), DESSENNE (A.), et VAN EFFENTERRE (H. et M.).
Messara XANTHOUDIDES (St.), *The Vaulted Tombs of Messara*, Liverpool 1924.
    For other sites see works by HOGARTH, BOSANQUET, DAWKINS, SEAGER, Miss BOYD, HALL, HOOD, HUTCHINSON, BOARDMAN, HAZZIDAKIS, XANTHOUDIDES, MARINATOS, PLATON, ALEXIOU.

III. Chronology

EVANS (Sir Arthur), *Essai de classification des époques de la civilisation minoenne*, Congrès d'Archéologie, 1906.
ABERG (N.), *Bronzezeitliche und früheisenzeitliche Chronologie*, *IV*, Griechenland, Stockholm 1933.
HUTCHINSON (R.), *Notes on Minoan Chronologie*, in Antiquity XXII, 1948, 61 ss.
Minoan Chronology Reviewed, in Antiquity, XXVIII, 1954, 155 ss.

MATZ (Fr.), *Zur ägäischen Chronologie der frühen Bronzezeit*, in Historia I., 1950, 173 ss.

LEVI (D.), *Classificazione della civiltà minoica*, in Parola del Passato, 1960, 81 ss.

PLATON (N.), *Chronologie minoenne* in Zervos (v. s.), 509 ss.

Chronologie de la Crète et des Cyclades à l'âge du bronze, in Bericht über den V. Internationalen Kongress für Vor- und Frühgeschichte, Hamburg 1958 (Berlin 1961), 671 ss.

SMITH (Sidn.), *Middle Minoan I and Babylonian Chronology* in Amer. Journal of Archaeol. 1945, I ss.

STUBBINGS (F.), *Chronology of the Aegean Bronze Age*, in Cambridge Anc. History I, 1962, VI, 69 ss.

WEINBERG (S.), *Relative Chronology of the Aegean in the Neolithic and the Early Bronze Age*, in Relative Chronologies in Old World Archaeology, 1954, 86 ss.

IV. Religion, Mythology

BANTI (L.), *Myth in pre-classical Art*, in Amer. Journal of Archaeol. 58, 1954, 302 ss.

EVANS (Sir Arthur), *Mycenaean Tree and Pillar Cult*, in Journal of Hellen. Studies XXI, 1901, 99 ss.

NILSSON (M.), *The Minoan-Mycenaean Religion*,[2] Lund 1950.

Geschichte der griechischen Religion,[2] I., Handbuch der Religionswissenschaft, V, 1950.

GUTHRIE (W.), *The Religion and Mythologie of the Greeks*, in Cambridge Ancient History II, 1961, 45 ss.

MATZ (Fr.), *Göttererscheinung und Kultbild im minoischen Kreta*, Abhandlung der Akademie Mainz, 1958.

PERSSON (A.W.), *The Religion of Greece in Prehistoric Times*, Sather Lectures, XVII, 1942.

PICARD (CH.), *Les Religions préhelléniques (Crète et Mycènes)*, Paris 1948.

V. Various Aspects of Art and Life

LORIMER (H.), *Homer and the Monuments*, London 1950.

BIESANTZ (H.), *Kretisch-mykenische Siegelbilder*, Marburg 1954.

KENNA (V.), *Cretan Seals*, Oxford 1960.

MATZ (Fr.), *Die frühkretischen Siegel*, Berlin-Leipzig 1928.

Torsion, Abhandlung der Akademie, Mainz 1951.

MARINATOS (Sp.), *La Marine crétomycénienne* in Bull. Corresp. Hellénique 57, 1933, 170 ss.

VI. Relations with Contemporary Civilizations

BURN (A.), *Minoans, Philistines and Greeks*, 1930.

KANTOR (H.I.), *The Aegean and the Orient in the Second Millennium B.C.*, Bloomington 1947.

MARINATOS (Sp.), *The Minoan and the Mycenaean Civilization and the Influence on the Mediterranean and Europe, VI*, Congress of Pre-and Protohistorical Sciences I, 1961.

PENDLEBURY (J.), *Aegyptiaca*, 1930.
Egypt and the Aegean in the Late Bronze Age, in Journal of Egyptian Archaeology 16, 1930.

VERCOUTTER (J.), *L'Egypte et le monde égéen préhellénique*, Cairo, 1956.
Egyptiens et Préhellènes, Paris, 1954.

VII. Language, Script, Race

CHADWICK (J.), *The Decipherment of Linear B*, Cambridge 1958.

PALMER (L.), *Mycenaeans and Minoans*, London 1961.

PALMER (L.), BOARDMAN (J.), *On the Knossos Tablets*, Oxford 1963.

STELLA (L.), *La civiltà Micenea nei documenti contemporanei*, Roma 1965.

VENTRIS (M.), CHADWICK (J.), *Documents in Mycenaean Greek*, Cambridge 1959.
Evidence for Greek dialect in the Mycenaean Archives, in Journal of Hellen. Studies 1953.

MYRES (J.L.), *Who were the Greeks?* Univ. of California, 1930.

VIII. The End of the Palaces and of Minoan Civilization

ANDRONIKOS (M.), *The Dorian Invasion and Archaeology*, in Ἑλληνικά 13, 1959, 45 ss.

MARINATOS (Sp.), *The Volcanic Destruction of Minoan Crete*, in Antiquity 13, 1939, 425 ss.

DESBOROUGH (V.), *The Last Mycenaeans and their Successors*, 1964.

LIST OF ILLUSTRATIONS

21 *Jar from the Royal Villa of Hagia Triada. c. 1500 B.C. (Photo. G. Bertin).*

22 *Palace of Phaistos: staircase in the west courtyard. (Photo. G. Bertin)*

23 *Wild goat. Bronze votive offering, dedicated to the sanctuary of Hagia Triada c. 1500 B.C. Museum of Heracleion. (Photo. G. Bertin)*

24 *Idem.*

25 *Figurine of an animal in terracotta, from Eastern Crete. c. 2000 B.C. Museum of Heracleion. (Photo. G. Bertin)*

26 *Minoan gold earrings from Knossos. Museum of Heracleion. (Photo. G. Bertin)*

27 *Minoan gold jewels from Knossos: fish and duck. Museum of Heracleion. (Photo. G. Bertin)*

28 *Biconical cup. Pyrgos style. From Pyrgos, Central Crete. c. 2500 B.C. Museum of Heracleion. (Photo. G. Bertin)*

29 *Goddess with snakes. Faience figure from the central sanctuary of the Palace of Knossos. c. 1600 B.C. Museum of Heracleion. (Photo. G. Bertin)*

30 *Worshippers. Terracotta figurines from the sanctuary of Piskokefalo, Sitia district, Eastern Crete. c. 1600 B.C. Museum of Heracleion. (Photo. G. Bertin)*

31 *Bronze statuettes from the Knossos district. c. 1500 B.C. Museum of Heracleion. Photo. G. Bertin)*

32 *Worshipper. Bronze statuette from the Royal Villa of Hagia Triada. c. 1500 B.C. Museum of Heracleion. (Photo. G. Bertin)*

33 *Acrobat. Figurine in ivory and gold from the Palace of Knossos. c. 1500 B.C. Museum of Heracleion. (Phoot. G. Bertin)*

34 *Rhyton in the form of a bull's head. Black steatite with inlays of rock crystal, jasper, and mother-of-pearl. Little Palace of Knossos. c. 1500 B.C. Museum of Heracleion. (Photo. G. Bertin)*

35 *Bronze statuette from the sacred cave of Psychro where Zeus was born. c. 1500 B.C. Museum of Heracleion. (Photo. G. Bertin)*

36 *Idem.*

37 *Votive offering in bronze, from Hagia Triada. c. 1500 B.C. Museum of Heracleion. (Photo. G. Bertin)*

38 *Rhyton in the form of a bull, with acrobats attached to the horns. From a domed tomb at Porti, Central Crete. c. 2100 B.C. Museum of Heracleion. (Photo. G. Bertin)*

39 *Rhyton in the form of a bull. Terracotta. From the island of Pseira in the Bay of Mirabello, Eastern Crete. c. 1500 B.C. Museum of Heracleion. (Photo. G. Bertin)*

40 *General view of the Palace of Zakro and the surrounding countryside. (Photo. Sosso Platon)*

41 *Central courtyard of the Palace of Zakro during the excavations, 1964. (Photo. Sosso Platon)*

42 *The treasury chamber at the Palace of Zakro. The partitions have been partially restored. (Photo. Sosso Platon)*

43 *Amphora with nine handles, in the marine style. Palace of Zakro. c. 1450 B.C. Museum of Heracleion. (Photo. G. Xylouris)*

44 *Amphora with crosspiece in the decorative style, seen from above. Palace of Zakro. c. 1450 B.C. Museum of Heracleion. (Photo. G. Xylouris)*

45 *The "nautilus jug" (cf. no 112), seen from above. Palace of Zakro. Museum of Heracleion. (Photo. G. Xylouris)*

46 *Porphyrite rhyton. Palace of Zakro. c. 1450 B.C. Museum of Heracleion. (Photo. G. Xylouris)*

47 *Stone rhyton with relief depicting a hilltop sanctuary. Palace of Zakro. c. 1450 B.C. Museum of Heracleion. (Photo. G. Xylouris)*

48 *Detail from the "rhyton of the sanctuary". Palace of Zakro. c. 1450 B.C. Museum of Heracleion. (Photo. G. Xylouris)*

49 *Ritual cup in veined marble. Palace of Zakro. c. 1450 B.C. Museum of Heracleion. (Photo. G. Xylouris)*

50 *Cup with plant decoration. Palace of Zakro. c. 1450 B.C. Museum of Heracleion. (Photo. G. Xylouris)*

51 *Ritual amphora in veined marble. Palace of Zakro. c. 1450 B.C. Museum of Heracleion. (Photo. G. Xylouris)*

52 *Faience nautilus. Palace of Zakro. c. 1450 B.C. Museum of Heracleion. (Photo. G. Xylouris)*

53 *Two-headed axe with elaborate plant decoration. Palace of Zakro. c. 1450 B.C. Museum of Heracleion. (Photo. G. Xylouris)*

54 *Small wine jugs discovered in the banqueting-hall of the Palace of Zakro, in situ, 1964. (Photo. Sosso Platon)*

55 **Lustral basin from the sanctuary, Palace of Zakro. (Photo. N. Platon)**

56 **Cup of olives found in the well of the fountain at the Palace of Zakro, 1964.** *(Photo. Sosso Platon)*

57 *Chamber of the bronze tripod, Palace of Zakro, during the excavations, 1964. (Photo. Sosso Platon)*

58 **Vase in the shape of a gourd, decorated with an octopus. Palaikastro, Eastern Crete. c. 1500 B.C. Museum of Heracleion. (Photo. G. Bertin)**

59 *Terracotta alabastron decorated with an octopus. Palace of Knossos. c. 1500 B.C. Museum of Heracleion. (Photo. G. Bertin)*

60 **Three-handled amphora decorated with octopuses in naturalistic style. Knossos, 1500 B.C. Museum of Heracleion. (Photo. G. Bertin)**

61 *Terracotta alabastron decorated with seabirds. Necropolis of Kalyvia, Phaistos. c. 1350 B.C. Museum of Heracleion. (Photo. G. Bertin)*

62 **Figurine of a bull, in bronze, from Praisos, Eastern Crete. c. 1400 B.C. Museum of Heracleion. (Photo. G. Bertin)**

63 **Bull. Bronze votive offering from Hagia Triada. c. 1500 B.C. Museum of Heracleion. (Photo. G. Bertin)**

64 *Idem.*

65 *Idem.*

66 **Horse. Bronze votive offering from Haiga Triada. c. 1500 B.C. Museum of Heracleion. (Photo. G. Bertin)**

67 **Rhyton in the form of a bull covered with a net. Terracotta. From: Isle of Pseira, Bay of Mirabello, Eastern Crete. c. 1500 B.C. Museum of Heracleion. (Photo. G. Bertin)**

68 **Bath-shaped sarcophagus, decorated with animals playing and suckling their young. From Gournia, Eastern Crete. c. 1350 B.C. Museum of Heracleion. (Photo. G. Bertin)**

69 **Terracotta sarcophagus decorated with papyri and seabirds. From Vasilika Anogeio, Central Crete. c. 1350 B.C. Museum of Heracleion.** *(Photo. G. Bertin)*

70 *Terracotta bull from the Palace of Phaistos. c. 1300 B.C. Museum of Heracleion. (Photo. G. Bertin)*

71   *Rhyton in the form of a bull's head. Black steatite. Palace of Zakro, Eastern Crete. c. 1500 B.C. Museum of Heracleion. (Photo. G. Bertin)*

72   *Gold pendant in the form of a bull's head. From Hagia Triada. c. 1500 B.C. Museum of Heracleion. (Photo. G. Bertin)*

73   *Gold pendant in the form of a recumbent lion. From Hagia Triada. c. 1500 B.C. Museum of Heracleion. (Photo. G. Bertin)*

74   *Gold jewels (diadem, hairpin) from the Isle of Mochlos. c. 2200 B.C. Museum of Heracleion.*

75   *Jug with raised spout, style of Hagios Onuphrios. From Kyparissi. c. 2500 Museum of Heracleion. (Photo. G. Bertin)*

76   *Base of a vase. Polychrome style of Kamares. Old Palace of Phaistos. 18th century B.C. Museum of Heracleion. (Photo. G. Bertin)*

77   *Vase in the form of a gourd. Polychrome style of Kamares. Old Palace of Knossos. 18th century B.C. Museum of Heracleion. (Photo. G. Bertin)*

78   *Vase in the form of a gourd in the polychrome style of Kamares, Knossos. 18th century B.C. Museum of Heracleion. (Photo. G. Bertin)*

79   *Two-handled vase, decorated with palm-trees, Polychrome style of Kamares. First Palace of Knossos. c. 1700 B.C. Museum of Heracleion. (Photo. G. Bertin)*

80   *Jar in Kamares style decorated with large fish caught in nets. First Palace of Phaistos. c. 1800 B.C. Museum of Heracleion. (Photo. G. Bertin)*

81   *Vase decorated with* fleurs de lys *in naturalistic style. Palace of Knossos. c. 1600 B.C. Museum of Heracleion. (Photo. G. Bertin)*

82   *Jar decorated with spirals. From Isle of Pseira, Bay of Mirabella, Eastern Crete. c. 1500 B.C. Museum of Heracleion. (Photo. G. Bertin)*

83   *Large jar decorated with two-headed axes. From Palace of Knossos. Palace style, c. 1400 B.C. Museum of Heracleion. (Photo. G. Bertin)*

84   *Seals made of hard semi-precious stones. Period of Second Palaces, 1580–1380 B.C. Museum of Heracleion. (Photo. G. Bertin)*

85   *Idem.*

86   *Engraved polychrome gem representing a wild goat at rest. c. 1600 B.C. Museum of Heracleion. (Photo. G. Bertin)*

87 *Porphyry lamp decorated with a wreath of leaves. From Isle of Pseira, Bay of Mirabello, Eastern Crete. c. 1500 B.C. Museum of Heracleion. (Photo. G. Bertin)*

88 *Polychrome vase with level spout in the Kamares style, from the First Palace of Phaistos. c. 1800 B.C. Museum of Heracleion. (Photo. G. Bertin)*

89 *Elliptical vase. Polychrome style of Kamares. Old palace of Phaistos. c. 1800 B.C. Museum of Heracleion. (Photo. G. Bertin)*

90 *Design from a polychrome plate in the Kamares style (pl. 91), showing two figures dancing round a deity. Old Palace of Phaistos. c. 1800 B.C. Museum of Heracleion. (Photo. G. Bertin)*

91 *Plate decorated with figures dancing round a deity. Polychrome style of Kamares. Old Palace of Phaistos. c. 1800 B.C. Museum of Heracleion (Photo. G. Bertin)*

92 *"Egg-shell" cups from the First Palace of Phaistos. Polychrome style of Kamares. c. 1800 B.C. Museum of Heracleion. (Photo. G. Bertin)*

93 *"Egg-shell" cup from the First Palace of Phaistos. Polychrome style of Kamares. c. 1800 B.C. Museum of Heracleion. (Photo. G. Bertin)*

94 *Vase with level spout, decorated with foliage. Royal villa of Hagia Triada. c. 1500 B.C. Museum of Heracleion. (Photo. G. Bertin)*

95 *Rhyton in rock crystal from the Palace of Zakro. c. 1450 B.C. Museum of Heracleion. (Photo. G. Bertin)*

96 *Worshipper. Terracotta, from the Sanctuary of the Two-Headed Axes at Knossos. c. 1250 B.C. Museum of Heracleion. (Photo. G. Bertin)*

97 *Jug with raised spout, decorated with plants. Second Palace of Phaistos. c. 1500 B.C. Museum of Heracleion. (Photo. G. Bertin)*

98 *Jug with raised spout, decorated with spirals. Palace of Knossos. c. 1500 B.C. Museum of Heracleion. (Photo. G. Bertin)*

99 *Jug with level spout, from Sklavokampos, Central Crete. c. 1500 B.C. Museum of Heracleion. (Photo. G. Bertin)*

100 *Cup with symbolic decoration: two headed axe and sacred knot. Palace of Phaistos. c. 1500 B.C. Museum of Heracleion. (Photo. G. Bertin)*

101 *Jug decorated with foliage. Palaikastro, Eastern Crete. c. 1500 B.C. Museum of Heracleion. (Photo. G. Bertin)*

102 *Left: small vase for cosmetics, in faience and gold. From Knossos. c. 1700 B.C. Museum of Heracleion. Right: miniature vase in stone, decorated with spirals. From the domed tomb of Platanos, in the Messara, Central Crete. c. 2100 B.C. Museum of Heracleion. (Photo. G. Bertin)*

103 *Cup decorated with so-called "mark of the viper" pattern. From a house at Knossos. c. 1500 B.C. Museum of Heracleion. (Photo. G. Bertin)*

104 *Three-handled amphora with helmet decoration, from a tomb at Katsamba, the ancient port of Knossos. c. 1400 B.C. Museum of Heracleion. (Photo. G. Bertin)*

105 *Detail of a stone rhyton decorated with wild goats and bearing the picture of a sanctuary. From Palace of Zakro. c. 1450 B.C. Museum of Heracleion. (Photo. G. Bertin)*

106 *Ritual chalice in veined marble. Palace of Zakro. c. 1450 B.C. Museum of Heracleion. (Photo. G. Bertin)*

107 *Worshippers. Bronze statuettes from the Royal Villa of Hagia Triada. c. 1500 and 1300 B.C. Museum of Heracleion. (Photo. G. Bertin)*

108 *Goddesses with head-dresses of sacred emblems. From Sanctuary of Gazi, Department of Heracleion. c. 1250 B.C. Museum of Heracleion. (Photo. G. Bertin)*

109 *Idem.*

110 *Terracotta statuette representing a goddess with snakes. From sanctuary of the rural Villa of Kanina, at Gortys, Central Crete. c. 1300 B.C. Museum of Heracleion. (Photo. G. Bertin)*

111 *Ritual chalice in obsidian. Palace of Zakro. c. 1450 B.C. Museum of Heracleion. (Photo. G. Bertin)*

112 *Jug with nautilus pattern. (cf. nᵒ 45) Palace of Zakro. Museum of Heracleion. (Photo. G. Bertin)*

113 *Gold ring with "granulated" pattern. Praisos, Eastern Crete. c. 1200 B.C. Museum of Heracleion. (Photo. G. Bertin)*

114 *Gold ring of unknown origin. Uprooting of the sacred tree. c. 1500 B.C. Museum of Heracleion. (Photo. G. Bertin)*

115 *Gold ring from the royal tomb of Isopata, Knossos. Invocation of the goddess. c. 1500 B.C. Museum of Heracleion. (Photo. G. Bertin)*

N. B. *References to illustrations are put in italics.*

THE TEXT AND ILLUSTRATIONS
IN THIS VOLUME WERE PRINTED
ON THE PRESSES OF NAGEL
PUBLISHERS IN GENEVA

FINISHED IN JANUARY 1966.
BINDING BY NAGEL PUBLISHERS,
GENEVA

PLATES ENGRAVED BY AMOR S.A.
GENEVA

LEGAL DEPOSIT NR. 376

PRINTED IN SWITZERLAND